COUNTDOWN AND COUNTUP
DAILY DEVOTIONAL FOR THE YEAR 2024

By
Pastor Zacchaeus I. OLORUNNIPA (PhD)

Countdown and Countup Daily Devotional for the Year 2024

Copyright © 2024 Pastor Zacchaeus I. OLORUNNIPA (PhD)

All rights reserved. No part of this book, "Countdown and Count up," may be reproduced, distributed, or transmitted in any form or by any means, including photocopying, recording, or other electronic or mechanical methods, without the prior written permission of the author, except in the case of brief quotations embodied in critical reviews and certain other noncommercial uses permitted by copyright law.

Scriptures marked KJV are taken from the KING JAMES VERSION (KJV): KING JAMES VERSION, public domain.

Scripture taken from the New King James Version®. Copyright ©1982 by Thomas Nelson. Used by permission. All rights reserved.

Scripture quotations marked (NIV) are taken from the Holy Bible, New International Version®, NIV®. Copyright © 1973, 1978, 1984, 2011 by Biblica, Inc.™ Used by permission of Zondervan.

All rights reserved worldwide. www.zondervan.com. The "NIV" and "New International Version" are trademarks registered in the United States Patent and Trademark Office by Biblica, Inc.™.

Unless otherwise indicated, all Scripture quotations are taken from the Holy Bible, New Living Translation, copyright © 1996, 2004, 2015 by Tyndale House Foundation. Used by permission of Tyndale House Publishers, Carol Stream, Illinois 60188. All rights reserved.

For questions, prayer requests, or permission requests to use quotes from this book, email the author at zacch51@yahoo.com
Download the "Countdown and Countup Daily Devotional for the Year" app from "App Store" and "Google Play Store"

Published by:
Eleviv Publishing Group
Xenia, OH 45385
info@elevivpublishing.com
www.elevivpublishing.com

ISBN: 978-1-952744-88-4

Printed in the United States of America

JANUARY

**Today is Jan 1, Day #1, in year 2024,
There are 365 more days remaining in year 2024.**

BECOMING BLESSED

SCRIPTURE: *"Blessed is the man Who walks not in the counsel of the ungodly, nor stands in the path of sinners, Nor sits in the seat of the scornful; But his delight is in the law of the Lord, And in His law he meditates day and night. He shall be like a tree Planted by the rivers of water, that brings forth its fruit in its season, Whose leaf also shall not wither; And whatever he does shall prosper."* **(Psalms 1:1-3 NKJV)**

PRAYER: Father, thank You for all Your past blessings and for sparing our lives to see the new year 2024. Oh Lord, please give us the grace to live holy, delighting in You and meditating day and night on Your word, so that we can continue to be blessed in year 2024 and beyond in Jesus' name **(Jer 4:2; Josh 1:8)**

ACTION: To delight in the Lord and be successful in life, study and meditate on God's world daily. Do so every day in 2024 and be blessed.

_____

_____

Today is Jan 2, Day #2, in year 2024,
There are 364 more days remaining in year 2024.

TRADING WITH GOD-GIVEN TALENTS

SCRIPTURE: *"He also who had received two talents came and said, 'Lord, you delivered to me two talents; look, I have gained two more talents besides them.' His Lord said to him, 'Well done, good and faithful servant; you have been faithful over a few things, I will make you ruler over many things. Enter into the joy of your Lord."* ***(Matt. 25:22-23 NKJV)***

PRAYER: Father, Your word declares, "Moreover it is required in stewards, that a man be found faithful ***(1 Cor, 4:2)***. Oh Lord, instead of burying my God-given talents (resources) please let me be faithful, meticulous and persevering in trading with them such that I can gain more than double the number of talents (resources) given to me

ACTION: Prayerfully ask God to reveal to you, your skill(s) and your areas of strength and how to harness your talents for enhancing your life and for glorifying God.

_____

_____

Today is, Jan 3, Day #3, in year 2024,
There are 363 more days remaining in year 2024.

FRUITFULNESS (1)

SCRIPTURE: *"He is like a tree planted beside streams - a tree that produces fruit in season and whose leaves do not wither. He succeeds in everything he does."* ***(Psa 1:3 GW)***

PRAYER: Father, please empower me to live holy, delight in Your law and meditate in it day and night so that I can be fruitful and be like 'a tree planted by the rivers of water, That brings forth its fruit in its season, whose leaf also shall not wither; And whatever he does shall prosper. ***(Psalms 1:2-3 NKJV)***

ACTION: Winning souls for God is one of the most valuable ways to fulfil the mandate of fruitfulness; throughout this year 2024 and beyond determine to abide in Jesus Christ and be fruitful ***(John 15:5-8)***

_____

_____

**Today is, Jan 4, Day #4 in year 2024,
There are 362 more days remaining in the year 2024**

BLESSING THE LORD AT 'VALLEY OF BERACHAH'

SCRIPTURE: *"And on the fourth day they assembled in the Valley of Berachah, for there they blessed the Lord; therefore, the name of that place was called The Valley of Berachah until this day."*

PRAYER: Father, the Valley of Berachah is where Jehoshaphat and his people went to celebrate and bless You when You gave them victory over their enemies from 3 nations *(2 Chron 20:1-28)*. Oh Lord, as You did for Jehoshaphat and Judah, please do for me and give me miraculous victory over all my enemies to provoke me to celebrate and bless You at my own 'Valley of Berachah' in the mighty name of Jesus

ACTION: Let us emulate Jehoshaphat by strengthening our prayer life with fasting and seeking the Lord and His help in dealing with our attackers *(2 Chron 20, NKJV)*

_____

_____

Today is, Jan 5, Day #5 in year 2024,
There are 361` more days remaining in year 2024.

WINNING WITH DIVINE WEAPONS

SCRIPTURE: *"He picked up five smooth stones from a stream and put them into his shepherd's bag. Then, armed only with his shepherd's staff and sling, he started across the valley to fight the Philistine." (1 Samuel 17:40 NLT)*

PRAYER: Father, this year and henceforth please give me wisdom and all the spiritual and physical weapons I need to conquer and overcome all my enemies as You gave David the wisdom and insights to choose the right weapons (five smooth stones and shepherd's staff and sling) with which he conquered and killed Goliath and defeated the Philistines the archenemy of Israel, *(1 Sam 17:1-40)*

ACTION: Study David's strategy used in overcoming Goliath and pray to God to give you wisdom like David's

_____

_____

**Today is, Jan 6, Day #6 in year 2024,
There are 360 more days remaining in year 2024.**

GOD MADE MAN TO BE VERY GOOD

SCRIPTURE: *"And God saw everything that he had made and that it was very good. There was evening, then morning—the sixth day."* ***(Genesis 1:31 GW)***

PRAYER: Father, thank You for your wonderful work of creation. Everything You created in each of the first 5 days of creation, You saw and described as 'good' ***(Gen 1:1-25)***. However, when God created human beings, 'man' (on the sixth day) He saw and described him as 'very good' ***(Gen 1:26-31)***. Oh Lord, I am a product of Your very good and wonderful work, therefore, I decree that Your goodness and mercy shall follow me all the days of my life and everything about me shall be very good forever in Jesus name

ACTION: God made you to be very good, always think of yourself to be very good and act so accordingly ***(Pro 23:7)***

_____

_____

**Today is, Jan 7, Day #7 in year 2024,
There are 359 more days remaining in year 2024**

PROMPT COMPLETION OF PROJECTS

SCRIPTURE: *"And on the seventh day God ended His work which He had done, and He rested on the seventh day from all His work which He had done"* ***(Gen. 2:2)***

PRAYER: Father, You finished the creation of the heavens and the earth only in seven days without any abandonment. Jesus Christ Your Son also successfully completed His work here on earth and declared 'It is finished' ***(John 19:30)***. Almighty God, in this year and henceforth, please give me the anointing to finish all my projects promptly without any delay, failure or abandonment in Jesus name.

ACTION: The God we serve *"faileth not'* ***(Zep 3:5)***, we his followers must determine not to fail

_____

_____

**Today is, Jan 8, Day #8 in year 2024,
There are 358 more days remaining in year 2024**

CIRCUMCISION OF JESUS CHRIST

SCRIPTURE: *"And when eight days were completed for the circumcision of the Child, His name was called Jesus, the name given by the angel before He was conceived in the womb." (Luke 2:21 NKJV)*

PRAYER: Lord Jesus, thank You for receiving circumcision on the 8th day after Your birth as a token of Your subjection to the law *(Gen 17:22; Gal 4-6)*. Father, please help us not to put confidence in the flesh, but, by faith, let us accept Jesus Christ as our Lord and Savior by whom we are entered into the new covenant, and according to that new covenant, *"..we are the circumcision, who worship by the Spirit of God and glory in Christ Jesus.." (Phil 3:3)*

ACTION: As Followers of Jesus Christ, we must keep the laws of God so that our circumcision can be profitable *(Rom 2:25)*

_____

_____

**Today is, Jan 9, Day #9 in year 2024,
There are 357 more days remaining in year 2024**

FORSAKE THE FOOLISH

SCRIPTURE: *"Forsake the foolish, and live; and go in the way of understanding." **(Proverbs 9:6)***

PRAYER: Father, Your word declares that the Fool:
(a) have said that there is no God *(Psa 24:1;53:1)*; (b) don't know God *(Jer 5:4)*, (c) is quick-tempered *(Pro14:17)*; (e) has mouth that is near destruction *(Pro 10:14)*. Please Lord, don't let me be unequally yoked together with unbelievers *(II Cor. 6:14 NKJV)*, so that I can live a meaningful life with undiluted understanding in Jesus name.

ACTION: Don't be a fool, avoid the foolish who says there is no God *(Psa. 14:1)*

**Today is, Jan 10, Day #10 in year 2024,
There are 356 more days remaining in year 2024.**

COMING OUT OF JORDAN

SCRIPTURE: *"And the people came up out of Jordan on the tenth day of the first month, and encamped in Gilgal, in the east border of Jericho."* ***(Jos. 4:19)***

PRAYER: Father, at Your directives the Israelites began their journey to the promised land on the 15th day of the FIRST month of a particular year ***(Exo 12:2)*** and, after 40 years less 5 days, the Israelites accomplished their goal and reached their destination (Canan) on the 10th day of the FIRST month of the year of arrival. Dear Lord, as we have started the journey of year 2024 on the first day of the first month, please help us to overcome all obstacles and reach the end of year 2024 safely on the 31st day of the 12th month of year 2024.

ACTION: Prayerfully claim the scripture in ***Psalm 32:8*** and believe that you shall make it safely to December 31st, year 2024 and

_____

_____

Today is Jan 11th Day #11 in year 2024, There are 355 more days remaining in year 2024

DELIVERANCE FROM DEMONIC DELAYS

SCRIPTURE: *"Normally it takes only eleven days to travel from Mount Sinai to Kadesh-barnea, going by way of Mount Seir."* **(Deut 1:2 NLT)**

PRAYER: Father, in this new year and thereafter please don't let me be a victim of demonic delays and/ or stagnation as did the Israelites who after their eleven days journey from Mount Sinai to Kadesh-barnea brought them to a few miles of entering the promised land, but still spent 38 years wandering up and down before they could reach their destination having been delayed by their rebellious attitude *(Num 32:13)*

ACTION: Let us pray regularly to cancel delays in all that we do

_____
_____

**Today is Jan 12th Day #12 in year 2024,
There are 354 more days remaining in year 2024**

GOOD HAND OF GOD

SCRIPTURE: *"Then we departed from the river of Ahava on the twelfth day (12th) of the first month, to go to Jerusalem. And the hand of our God was upon us, and He delivered us from the hand of the enemy and from ambush along the road." (Ezra 8:31 NKJV)*

PRAYER: Father, thank You for Your good hand *(Ezra 7:9; 8:18; Neh.2:8,18)*. As You did for Ezra, and Nehemiah and their respective entourages please Lord, in all our journeys and other undertakings this day, year and henceforth, let Your hand be upon us to deliver us from the hands of our enemies and from ambush along the road and ensure safe and successful accomplishment of our mission in Jesus name *(Ezra 7; Neh. 2; Deut. 33:27)*

ACTION: Pray to God to grave you in His good hand *(Isa. 49:16)*

_____

_____

**Today is Jan 13th Day #13 in year 2024,
There are 353 more days remaining in year 2024**

HAMAN'S DEATH DECREE BACKFIRED

SCRIPTURE: *"Then the king's scribes were called on the thirteenth day of the first month, and a decree was written according to all that Haman commanded—to the king's satraps, to the governors who were over each province, to the officials of all people, to every province according to its script, and to every people in their language. In the name of King Ahasuerus, it was written and sealed with the king's signet ring. And the letters were sent by couriers into all the king's provinces, to destroy, to kill, and to annihilate all the Jews, both young and old, little children and women, in one day, on the thirteenth day of the twelfth month, which is the month of Adar, and to plunder their possessions."* **(Esther 3:12-13 NKJV)**.

PRAYER: Father, please let every evil agenda and/or death sentence orchestrated against us backfire to the plotter as it happened to Haman who died in the gallows he plotted and prepared for Mordecai *(Est. 7:10)*. Also, Lord, as You overturned the death decrees of other Jews Haman wanted killed, please overturn every plan of Satan to kill any of us in Jesus' name *(Esther 8, 9, 10)*

ACTION: Pray that any weapon of death aimed at you shall fail

**Today is Jan 14th Day #14 in year 2024,
There are 352 more days remaining in year 2024.**

THE LORD'S PASSOVER

SCRIPTURE: *"In the fourteenth day of the first month at even is the Lord's Passover"* **(Lev. 23:5)**

PRAYER: PRAYER: Father, in this first month of this year, please set us free from anything that has held us in captivity (Satan, sins, sickness, stagnation, poverty, debts, unable to get married, marital conflicts, joblessness, bareness, academic problems, etc,) as You freed the Israelites (after they ate the Passover meal) from the land of Egypt where they were held for about 400 years in captivity and servitude *(Lev 23; Exo 12)*

ACTION: If you have given your life to Jesus Christ, prayerfully partake in taking the Holy Communion wherever and whenever it is properly administered. Pray that Jesus Christ will set you free indeed

_____

_____

**Today is Jan 15th, Day #15 in year 2024,
There are 351 more days remaining in year 2024**

ESCAPING TRIUMPHANTLY FROM THE ENEMIES

SCRIPTURE: *"They set out from Rameses on the fifteenth day of the first month; on the day after the Passover the Israelites moved out triumphantly in the sight of all the Egyptians, while the Egyptians were burying all their firstborn whom the Lord had struck down among them. Upon their gods the Lord also executed judgments." (Numbers 33:3-4 AMP)*

PRAYER: Father, on this 15th day of the first month and henceforth, please let me escape triumphantly from all 'Egyptian-like' enemies as You made it happen at Rameses where on the 15th day of the first month *"..the children of Israel went out with an high hand in the sight of all the Egyptians"(Num. 33:3, KJV)*

ACTION: Pray that all enemies pursuing you will be smitten by God and they will flee from you in 15 ways *(Deut 28:7)*

_____

_____

**Today is Jan 16th, Day #16 in year 2024,
There are 350 more days remaining in year 2024**

CASTING ALL CARES ON CHRIST

SCRIPTURE: *"Commit your works to the Lord, And your thoughts will be established." **(Proverbs 16:3 NKJV)***

PRAYER: Father thank You for Your care for me *(1 Pet 5:7)* and Your promise to help me *(Isa 42:10)*. Please Lord, this year and henceforth let me continue to depend upon You alone for direction and success; in all my works and undertakings in Jesus name.

ACTION: Do what **Proverbs 3:5** says: *'Trust in the Lord with all thine heart; and lean not unto thine own understanding.'*

_____

_____

**Today is Jan 17th, Day #17 in year 2024,
There are 349 more days remaining in year 2024**

FEROCIOUS FLOOD

SCRIPTURE: *"In the six hundredth year of Noah's life, ...,the seventeenth day of the month, on that day all the fountains of the great deep were broken up, and the windows of heaven were opened. The waters prevailed fifteen cubits upward, and the mountains were covered. And all flesh died that moved on the earth: ...,birds and ......All in whose nostrils was the breath of the spirit of life, all that was on the dry land, died.....Only Noah and those who were with him in the ark remained alive." **(Gen. 7:11, 20-23 NKJV)**

PRAYER: Father, the flood that destroyed the whole world (excepting Noah and his family) began on day 17th of the month. Please Lord, have mercy and forgive us our sins, individually and collectively and put an end to various disasters that have been plaguing our world in recent times (e.g. Corona virus, excessive fire outbreaks, storms, tornadoes, ferocious floods, overwhelming snow fall, excessive heat, wars, kidnapping and indiscriminate killings of human beings, etc). Dear Lord, our refuge, keep us in Your ark of safety, and help us to be ready for Your return in Jesus' name.

ACTION: Pray that sins will not sink you and all yours

Today is January 18th, Day #18 in year 2024.
There are 348 days remaining in year 2024

LOSING HOPE AND CONFIDENCE IN THE LORD?

SCRIPTURE: *"He hath stripped me of my glory and taken the crown from my head."* ***(Job 19:9)***

PRAYER: Father, Your word declares that You will never leave me nor forsake me ***(Heb 13:5)*** Please Lord, don't let life's circumstances and what people say discourage me and provoke me to make wrong judgment and unfounded accusation about You and Your role in my life in Jesus name

ACTION: As believers in the Lord Let us thank God for His ever presence and protection for us ***(Isa 43:1-4)***

_____

_____

**Today is January 19th, Day #19 in year 2024.
There are 347 days remaining in year 2024**

SAVING THE SEEKER

SCRIPTURE: *"And when Jesus came to the place, he looked up, and saw him, and said unto him, Zacchaeus, make haste, and come down; for today I must abide at thy house., 9 And Jesus said unto him, This day is salvation come to this house, for so much as he also is a son of Abraham."* ***(Luke 19: 6, 9)***

PRAYER: Father, thank You for Your faithfulness to Your promise: *"..,ye shall seek me, and find me, when ye shall search for me with all your heart"* ***(Jer. 29:13)***; please let those yet to receive Jesus as their Lord and Savior seek and search for Him desperately as did Zacchaeus who caught Jesus' attention by running before Him, and climbed up into a sycamore tree to see Him ***(Luke 19: 1-10)***.

ACTION: Pray for revival that will draw multitude of unbelievers to have a yearning to seek Jesus Christ as did Zacchaeus

_____
_____

**Today is Jan 20th, Day #20 in the year 2024.
There are 346 days remaining in year 2024.**

DEVIL IS A DECEIVER

SCRIPTURE: *"And cast him into the bottomless pit, and shut him up, and set a seal upon him, that he should deceive the nations no more, till the thousand years should be fulfilled: and after that he must be loosed a little season."* ***(Rev. 20:3)***

PRAYER: Father, '..deliver us from evil' ***(Matt 6:13)*** for he is a deceiver ***(Gen 3:1-7, 2 Cor 4:4, Rev 20:3)***. Please Lord, give us the power to resist the devil such that he will flee from us ***(James 4:7)***.

ACTION: Let's cry to God daily to cast the devil into the bottomless pit to terminate his business of deceiving the nations

_____

_____

**Today is Jan 21st, Day #21 in year 2024,
There are 345 more days remaining in year 2024.**

PRAISING THE LORD'S POWER

SCRIPTURE: *"Be exalted, O Lord, in Your own strength! We will sing and praise Your power." **(Psa.21:13 NKJV)***

PRAYER: Father, please give us the grace and reasons to praise You for Your power as did king David when You gave him: salvation, victory over all his enemies, his heart's desire, blessings of goodness; You set a crown of pure gold upon his head, Length of days forever and ever, Honor and majesty, Your presence, etc. *(Psa. 21:1-6 NKJV)*
Oh Lord, please fill my mouth with songs of joy in praising You in Jesus name.

ACTION: Emulate David who declares *"I will bless the Lord at all times; His praise shall continually be in my mouth." **(Psa. 34:1)***

_____

_____

**Today is Jan 22nd, Day #22 in year 2024,
There are 344 more days remaining in year 2024.**

DECLARING DECREES

SCRIPTURE: *"Thou shalt also decree a thing, and it shall be established unto thee: and the light shall shine upon thy ways."* **(Job 22:28, KJV)**

PRAYER: Father, thank You for giving us the privilege of using decrees (faith-based commands or authoritative order) in prayers; as Your word declares, *"Say to them, 'As I live,' says the Lord, 'just as you have spoken in My hearing, so I will do to you:"* **(Num. 14:28 NKJV)**. Therefore, in Jesus' name I decree that:

1. Thanksgiving and praising God shall not depart from my mouth.
2. I will live and not die to declare the works of God.
3. I will make heaven together with all members of my family.
4. Through me, many souls shall be saved and ready to be raptured.
5. I will prosper body, soul, in Spirit, financially and in all positive areas
6. The blessing of God that maketh rich and add no sorrow is my portion.
7. No weapon fashioned against me shall prosper.

ACTION: Prayerfully make decreeing as part of your daily prayer

Today is Jan 23rd, Day #23 in year 2024, There are 343 more days remaining in year 2024.

JEHOAHAZ'S SHORT-LIVED REIGN IN JERUSALEM

SCRIPTURE: *"Jehoahaz was twenty-three years old when he became king, and he reigned three months in Jerusalem." (II Chronicles 36:2 NKJV)*

PRAYER: Father, please bless our children and let them serve You even better than their parents. Don't let our children be like 3 of the children of Josiah called the same name (title) Jehoahaz. The third Jehoahaz (also known as Shallum *(1 Chron 3:15)* came to the throne at age 23 and *"did evil in the eyes of the LORD, just as his predecessors has done" (2 Kings 23:32, NIV)*. Shallum only reigned for three months in Jerusalem before Pharaoh deported him in chains to Egypt where he later died *(2 Kings 23:31-35)*.
Oh Lord, please turn the hearts of our rulers away from greed, corruption and other evil practices to righteous lifestyles so that we, Your people can rejoice, in Jesus name *(Proverbs 29:2)*

ACTION: Development of Leadership skills must be incorporated into the training of our children and all young people in the ministry.

Today is January 24th, Day #24 in year 2024.
There are 342 days remaining in year 2024.

HOW TO BUILD A HOUSE

SCRIPTURE: *"Through wisdom is an house builded; and by understanding it is established: 4 And by knowledge shall the chambers be filled with all precious and pleasant riches" (Pro 24: 3-4)*

PRAYER: Father, please give me divine wisdom knowledge and understanding to build spiritual and physical houses that will meet Your standard for habitation, in Jesus' name

ACTION: We must prayerfully seek wisdom from God daily in building and maintaining both our spiritual and physical 'houses'

_____

_____

**Today is Jan 25th, Day #25 in the year 2024.
There are 341 more days remaining in year 2024.**

JEHOSHAPHAT'S REIGN IN JERUSALEM

SCRIPTURE: *"..So Jehoshaphat…ruled in Jerusalem for 25 years. His mother's name was Azubah. She was the daughter of Shilhi. Jehoshaphat lived in the good way that his father Asa had lived. He only did things that the Lord says are right. But he did not remove all the altars that were on the hills. The people still did not want to be completely faithful to the God of their ancestors." (2 Chro 20:31-33 EASY)*

PRAYER: Father, please give us rulers like Jehoshaphat who will:
(a) fear You and do only things that are right in Your sight
(b) seek and follow Godly counsel in dealing with issues such as how to fight against the enemies *(2 Chron 20: 3-5)*, (c) will allow and encourage freedom of people to worship, praise and magnify God *(2 Chron 20:13)*. Oh Lord, don't let our rulers engage in or support evil altars, idol worship and Ungodly alliances as did Jehoshaphat

ACTION: Pray that God will give us good and righteous rulers who will do things that are right in the sight of God.

_____

_____

**Today is Jan 26th, Day #26 in year 2024,
There are 340 more days remaining in year 2024.**

DANGER IN GETTING DRUNK

SCRIPTURE: *"When Asa had been king of Judah for 26 years, Baasha's son Elah became king of Israel. He ruled as king in Tirzah for two years. Zimri was one of Elah's officers. He had authority over half of Elah's chariots. Zimri decided to kill King Elah. One day, Elah was in the home of a man called Arza, an officer who had authority over the king's palace in Tirzah. Elah was drinking too much wine and he became drunk. Zimri came in to Arza's house. He hit Elah and he killed him. When this happened, Asa had been king of Judah for 27 years. Zimri made himself king instead of Elah." (1 Kings 16:8-10 EASY)*

PRAYER: Father, Your word says, *"....woe to those who are overcome with wine!" **(Isaiah 28:1 NKJV)**;* and that *"Wine is a mocker, strong drink is raging: and whosoever is deceived thereby is not wise" **(Proverbs 20:1)***. Please Lord, help us not to be overcome by what we eat or drink as it happened to King Elah of Israel; Noah **(Gen 9:20-26)**; Nabal **(1 Sam. 25:32-38)**; Amnon **(2 Sam. 13: 28-29)**, etc.

ACTION: Prayerfully avoid eating what might 'eat and kill you

_____

_____

Today is Jan 27th, Day #27 in year 2024,
There are 339 more days remaining in year 2024.

LORD IS MY LIGHT, SALVATION AND STRENGTH OF MY LIFE

SCRIPTURE: *"The Lord is my light and my salvation; Whom shall, I fear? The Lord is the strength of my life; Of whom shall I be afraid?"* ***(Psalms 27:1 NKJV)***

PRAYER: Father, I thank You for You are everything to me (light, salvation, strength, shield, helper, guide, guard, provider, deliverer, advocate, etc), for in You I live, and move, and have my being *(Acts 17:28)*. Therefore, in the spirit of *Psalm 27*, I decree and declare that:
I shall not fear or be afraid; all my wicked enemies and foes wanting to eat my flesh shall stumble and fall; as my body is Your Temple *(2 Cor 6:19)*, nothing shall separate me from You and Your Temple; in time of trouble You shall hide me in Your pavilion; my head shall be lifted up above mine enemies round about me in Jesus mighty name.

ACTION: Devote quality time daily to thank and praise God for everything He is to you

_____

_____

**Today is Jan 28th, Day #28 in year 2024,
There are 338 more days remaining in year 2024.**

CONFESSING VERSUS COVERING SINS

SCRIPTURE: *"He who covers his sins will not prosper, But whoever confesses and forsakes them will have mercy." (Proverbs 28:13 NKJV)*

PRAYER: Father, Your word makes it clear that all have sinned *(Rom 3:23)*, and that *"…the wages of sin is death; but the gift of God is eternal life through Jesus Christ our Lord" (Rom. 6:23)*. Oh Lord, let those who have not yet received salvation of Jesus Christ stop covering their sins and accept the salvation offered by Jesus Christ *(Rom 10:9)*

ACTION: Intercede daily for the salvation of all unsaved members of your family (if any)

_____

_____

Today is Jan 29th, Day #29 in year 2024,
There are 337 more days remaining in year 2024.

GIVING UNTO GOD

SCRIPTURE: *"Give unto the LORD, O ye mighty, give unto the LORD glory and strength." **(Psalms 29:1)***

PRAYER: Father, thank You for loving us and giving us Your Son, Jesus Christ as a ransom and price for our eternal life *(John 3:16)*; please help us to obey You and love You *(Deut. 28:1-2; Mark 12:30)* and to always be generous in giving You thanks and glory and in serving You with our time, talents and treasures in Jesus name *(Mal. 3:10-12)*

ACTION: Give to God, remembering that it is more blessed to give than to receive *(Acts 20:35)*

_____

_____

**Today is Jan 30th, Day #30 in year 2024,
There are 336 more days remaining in year 2024**

JAIR THE RICH ISRAELI JUDGE

SCRIPTURE: *"After Tola, Jair of Gilead became Israel's leader. He led Israel for 22 years. He had 30 sons. They rode on 30 donkeys, and they ruled 30 towns in Gilead. These towns are still called Havvoth-Jair (Jair's villages)." (Judges 10:3-4 EASY)*

PRAYER: Father, make us fruitful and relevant in serving You and humanity. As you blessed Jair of Israel with 30 successful sons, please give children to those who are in need of them and let all our children be highly successful in their vocations in Jesus name.

ACTION: Pray for the success of those waiting to have their own children

_____

_____

**Today is Jan 31st, Day #31 in year 2024,
There are 335 more days remaining in year the 2024.**

JOSIAH'S REIGN AS KING OF JUDAH

SCRIPTURE: *"Josiah was eight years old when he became king. He ruled as king in Jerusalem for 31 years....Josiah did things that the Lord said were right. He lived in the good ways of his ancestor, King David. He did not turn away from the Lord's teaching in any way."*
(2 Kings 22:1-2 EASY)

PRAYER: Father, please give us the grace to emulate king Josiah in terms of doing what is right in Your sight, ensuring Your house is well maintained, Your word is read and obeyed and living a life of humility in Jesus name ***(2 kings 22)***.

ACTION: Give thanks to God for safety thus far as first month of year 2024 ends today. Pray for smooth transition into February month.

_____

_____

FEBRUARY

Today is Feb 1st, Day #32 in year 2024,
There are 334 more days remaining in year 2024.

RAISING A FAMILY

SCRIPTURE: *"Reu was 32 years old when he became the father of Serug. After he became the father of Serug, Reu lived 207 years and had other sons and daughters. Serug was 30 years old when he became the father of Nahor. After he became the father of Nahor, Serug lived 200 years and had other sons and daughters."* **(Gen. 11:20-23 GW)**

PRAYER: Father, thank You for the gift of children. When our young people are ripe for marriage and raising families, please give them the grace to marry the right way and to be fruitful in their marriages, like Rue, Serug, Nahor, Abram, etc. *(Gen 11: 10-32. KJV)*

ACTION: Pray for successful marriage and fruitfulness in your family from generation to generation

_____

_____

**Today is Feb 2nd, Day #33 in the year 2024,
There are 333 more days remaining in year 2024.**

SURROUNDED BY GOD'S SHIELD

SCRIPTURE: *"But thou, O LORD, art a shield for me; My glory, and the lifter up of mine head."* ***(Psalm 3:3 KJV).***

PRAYER: Father, as You protected David against all his enemies (internal and external), please in Jesus name, do the same for me and be:
(1) A Shield for me; (2) My Glory; (3) The Lifter up of mine head; (4) My Guide; (5) My Sustainer; (6) My very present help; (7) My all in all.

ACTION: Shout 33 Hallelujahs in praise to God for being your shield.

_____

_____

Today is Feb 3rd, Day #34 in year 2024,
There are 332 more days remaining in year 2024.

SEEKING GOD FOR SOLUTIONS

SCRIPTURE: *"I sought the LORD, and he heard me, And delivered me from all my fears."* **(Psalm 34:4 KJV)**

PRAYER: Father, instead of been fearful and anxious about our concerns and issues of life, give us the grace to trust You enough to hand them over to You in prayer as Your word declares: *"Give all your worries and cares to God, for he cares about you."* **(1 Pet 1:5 NLT)**. Oh Lord turn all my anxieties to advantages in Jesus name.

ACTION: Prayerfully obey the injunction: *"Be anxious for nothing, but in everything by prayer and supplication, with thanksgiving, let your requests be made known to God;"* **(Philippians 4:6)**

_____
_____

**Today is Feb 4th, Day #35 in year 2024,
There are 331 more days remaining in year 2024.**

GIVING BEST OFFERING TO GOD

SCRIPTURE: *"Moses said to the whole Israelite community, "This is what the Lord has commanded: From what you have, take an offering for the Lord. Everyone who is willing is to bring to the Lord an offering of gold, silver and bronze, etc." (Exodus 35:4-9 NIV)*

PRAYER: Father, please give us the grace to willingly give You the best offering for You gave us Your best, Your Son *(John 3:16)*. Furthermore, Your word declares: *"...A man can receive nothing unless it has been given to him from heaven." (John 3:27 NKJV)*, and that every good gift and every perfect gift is from You *(James 1:17 NKJV)*. Lord, please help me to give You the best to get the best *(Luke 6:38; Gal. 6:7)*

ACTION: Prayerfully try it: It is more blessed to give than to receive *(Acts 20:35b)*

_____

_____

Today is Feb 5th, Day #36 in year 2024,
There are 330 more days remaining in year 2024.

GREATNESS OF GOD

SCRIPTURE: *"Certainly, God is so great that he is beyond our understanding. The number of his years cannot be counted." (Job 36:26 GW)*

PRAYER: Father, thank You for Your unsearchable greatness as exemplified in numerous ways including:
(a) You are everlasting and numberless in terms of age.
(b) Your formation of all things without partiality *(Pro 26:10)*.
(c) Your mightiness and awesomeness *(Deut 10;17)*
(d) Your supremacy above all gods *(Psa 95:3)*
(e) Your miracles, wonders and signs *(Acts 2:22)*,
(f) You do mrvelous things without number *(Job 5:9)*, etc.
Oh, Great God, please let the praise of You fill our mouths always.

ACTION: Start each day with praise and prayer to the Great God

_____
_____

**Today is Feb 6th, Day #37 in year 2024,
There are 329 more days remaining in year 2024.**

GUIDANCE BY GOD

SCRIPTURE: *"Let the Lord be your guide into the future. Trust in him and he will help you."* ***(Psalms 37:5 EASY).***

PRAYER: Father, please continue to guide, lead and direct my future in this year 2024 and beyond for Your way is perfect ***(Psa 18:30)***; and Your word declares: *"...the ways of man are before the eyes of the LORD, and he pondereth all his goings. **(Pro. 5:21)***. Oh Lord, You are the One that knows the way to the 'wilderness', please let me trust, obey and follow You as You lead me in the path of righteousness, success, peace, joy, prosperity, etc, and to the expected end of Your heavenly Kingdom in Jesus name

ACTION: Let us seek God's guidance in everything we do.

_____

_____

**Today is Feb 7th, Day #38 in year 2024,
There are 328 more days remaining in year 2024.**

HELPER OF THE HELPLESS

SCRIPTURE: *"There is a pool near the Sheep Gate in Jerusalem. Its name in the Jewish language is Bethesda. Round the pool, ... A large number of sick people were lying in these places...They were waiting for when the water started to move. An angel would go down into the pool at certain times and move the water about. When that happened, all the sick people tried to get into the pool. The first person who got into the water became well, whatever his illness was. One man who was lying there had been ill for 38 years. Jesus saw this man. He knew that the man had been ill like this for a very long time. So, he asked the man, 'Do you want to get well?' The sick man said, 'Sir, I do not have anyone who will help me. I need somebody who will put me into the pool. When the water starts to move, I try to get in. But someone else always gets in before me.' Then Jesus said to him, 'Stand up! Pick up your mat and walk.' The man became well immediately. He picked up his mat and he walked....."* **(John 5:2-9 EASY)**

PRAYER: Father, the very Present help and the Helper of the helpless, please help us and heal us today and terminate all protracted problems in our lives as You did for the man at the Pool of Bethesda who was infirmed for 38 years.

ACTION: Touch any part of your body that has any ailment and cry to Jesus to help you by healing you

Today is Feb 8th, Day #39 in year 2024, There are 327 more days remaining in year 2024.

SUFFERING FOR GOD'S SAKE

SCRIPTURE: *"At five different times, the Jewish leaders punished me with whips. Each time they hit me 39 times. Three times the Romans punished me with sticks. People threw stones at me to kill me once. Three times I have been on ships that broke in the sea. Once I was in the sea for a night and a day. ...."* ***(2 Cor.11:24-26 EASY)***

PRAYER: Father, thank You for Your word that forewarns us that, *"...all that will live godly in Christ Jesus shall suffer persecution."* ***(2 Timothy 3:12)***; Lord Jesus, please give us the grace, the strength and the resilience to serve You diligently to the end without quitting because of persecution as You did, and as Apostle Paul did despite the persecutions he faced as indicated in today's lead scripture above.

Father, if and whenever we face persecution in doing Your work, help us to find solace in Your promise that says, *"Blessed are ye, when men shall revile you, and persecute you, and shall say all manner of evil against you falsely, for my sake. Rejoice, and be exceeding glad: for great is your reward in heaven: for so persecuted they the prophets which were before you"* ***(Matthew 5:11-12, KJV)***

ACTION: Count it all joy when you suffer for Jesus Christ ***(1 Pet 4:13)***

**Today is Feb 9th, Day #40 in the year 2024,
There are 326 more days remaining in year 2024.**

FED BY GOD, THE FATHER

SCRIPTURE: *"The Israelites ate the manna for 40 years, until they had finished their journey in the desert. After those 40 years, they arrived at the edge of Canaan."* (Exodus 16:35 EASY)

PRAYER: Father, Your word declares that, *"The young lions do lack, and suffer hunger: but they that seek the LORD shall not want any good thing." **(Psalms 34:10)**.* Oh Lord don't let us lack any good thing or suffer hunger; please give us the grace to seek and serve You and be fed by You as You did for the whole nation of Israel in the wilderness for 40 years ***(Exo 16)***, and Elijah the Prophet whom You miraculously fed using raven birds and a widow woman ***(1 Kings 17: 1-16)***

ACTION: Pray to God to feed you till you want no more

_____

_____

**Today is Feb 10th, Day #41 in year 2024,
There are 325 more days remaining in year 2024.**

HELPING THE POOR AND THE HELPLESS

SCRIPTURE: *"Those who help the poor succeed will get many blessings. When trouble comes, the Lord will save them. The Lord will protect them and save their lives. He will bless them in this land. He will not let their enemies harm them. When they are sick in bed, the Lord will give them strength and make them well!" **(Psalms 41:1-3 ERV)***

PRAYER: Father, Your word declares *"He who has pity on the poor lends to the Lord, And He will pay back what he has given." **(Pro. 19:17 NKJV)***. Please Lord, empower and position us to help the needy and the poor and, as it pleases You, bless us in many ways including:
Preserving and keeping us alive; Not delivering us to the will of our enemies; Sustaining and strengthening us to recover from all infirmities and sicknesses; Ensuring that all our own needs are met in Jesus' name. Amen. ***(Psalms 41:1-3 NKJV)***

ACTION: Periodically, try to help someone meet special need(s) in their life

_____

_____

**Today is Feb 11th, Day #42 in year 2024,
There are 324 more days remaining in year 2024.**

SOUL THAT CRAVES FOR GOD

SCRIPTURE: *"As the deer pants for the water brooks, So pants my soul for You, O God." **(Psalms 42:1 NKJV)***

PRAYER: Father, Your word declares. *"....You shall love the Lord your God with all your heart, with all your soul, with all your strength, and with all your mind...." **(Luke 10:27 NKJV).***
Father, please command and condition my soul to crave, thirst and hunger for You passionately without wavering in Jesus name

ACTION: Evaluate yourself which you crave more for, between God and food?

_____

_____

**Today is Feb 12th, Day #43 in year 2024,
There are 323 more days remaining in year 2024.**

CREATED BY GOD AND CALLED BY CHRIST?

SCRIPTURE: *"Everyone who is called by My name, Whom I have created for My glory; I have formed him, yes, I have made him."* **(Isaiah 43:7 NKJV)**

PRAYER: Father, thank You for creating, forming and making us in Your own image and sending Your Son Jesus Christ into the world to call us out of darkness into His Marvelous light *(1 Peter 2:9)*. Almighty God, as You have created and called me, please let my life glorify You in Jesus name.

ACTION: Pray that the call of God on you will not be in vain in Jesus.

_____

_____

Today is Feb 13th, Day #44 in year 2024,
There are 322 more days remaining in year 2024.

PREVAILING OVER ENEMIES BY GOD'S POWER

SCRIPTURE: *"Because of your power, we can knock down our enemies. Because of your strength, we can beat them down."* **(Psalms 44:5 EASY)**

PRAYER: Father, by Your power and strength let me prevail and be victorious over all my enemies in Jesus name

ACTION: Pray that the call of God on you will not be in vain in Jesus.

_____

_____

**Today is Feb 14th, Day #45 in year 2024,
There are 321 more days remaining in year 2024.**

WARNINGS FOR RULERS WHO ARE WICKED

SCRIPTURE: *"The Almighty Lord says this: Rulers of Israel, stop cheating my people and making them suffer! You have done enough bad things! Instead, do things that are right and fair. Stop chasing my people off their land. That is what the Almighty Lord says."* **(Ezekiel 45:9 EASY)**

PRAYER: Father, Your word declares, *"The king's heart is in the hand of the LORD, as the rivers of water: he turneth it whithersoever he will"* **(Proverbs 21:1, KJV).** Oh Righteous God, please turn the hearts of leaders and rulers of nations from wicked deeds such as greed, exploitation, cheating, exactions, violence, and other actions that can create suffering and hardships for their subjects. Let these rulers do what is right in Your sight, otherwise remove them in Jesus name.

ACTION: Pray that wicked, corrupt and people who do not have the fear of God will not be chosen as rulers

_____

_____

Today is Feb 15th, Day #46 in year 2024,
There are 320 more days remaining in year 2024.

PROVOKING GOD'S GRACIOUS PROMISES

SCRIPTURE: *"So Israel took his journey with all that he had, and came to Beersheba, and offered sacrifices to the God of his father Isaac. Then God spoke to Israel in the visions of the night, and said, "Jacob, Jacob!" And he said, "Here I am." So He said, "I am God, the God of your father; do not fear to go down to Egypt, for I will make of you a great nation there. I will go down with you to Egypt, and I will also surely bring you up again;"* **(Genesis 46:1-4 NKJV)**

PRAYER: Father, Your word declares, *"Offer the sacrifices of righteousness, and put your trust in the LORD"* **(Psalms 4:5)**; Oh God, help me to trust You and offer appropriate sacrifices to You as did Jacob that I may also receive gracious promises from You akin to those released to Jacob in today's lead scripture *(Gen, 46:1-7)*.
In all my journeys this day and henceforth please go with me, protect me and bless me greatly in Jesus' name.

ACTION: Give thanks to God who keeps all His promises *(2 Cor 1:20, Josh. 23:14)*

**Today is Feb 16th, Day #47 in year 2024,
There are 319 more days remaining in year 2024.**

WONDERFUL GOD THAT RULES OVER THE WORLD

SCRIPTURE: *"The Lord, the Most High God, is wonderful. He is the great King who rules over the whole earth." **(Psa. 47:2 EASY)***

PRAYER: Father, thank You for who You are and Your amazing attributes which are beyond description. LORD, Your are: Wonderful, the Highest, the Great King, Omnipotent; Omnipresent, Omniscient, the mightiest of all emperors, the Prince of peace etc; Dear Lord please exercise Your Sovereignty all over the whole world and let there be peace like a river and righteousness as the waves of the sea, in Jesus name *(Isaiah 48:18)*

ACTION: Pray that Godly agenda that will give room for peace will prevail in all the countries of the world

_____

_____

**Today is Feb 17th, Day #48 in year 2024,
There are 318 more days remaining in year 2024.**

GOD IS FOR EVER OUR GUIDE

SCRIPTURE: *"For this God is our God for ever and ever; he will be our guide even to the end." **(Psalms 48:14 NIV)***

PRAYER: Father, thank You for Your promise never to leave us or forsake us *(Heb 13:5b)* and to be our guide even to the end. Please Lord, give us the grace to love You and be so committed and connected to You like Apostle Paul so that we too can declare that, *"neither death nor life, neither angels nor demons, neither the present nor the future, nor any powers, neither height nor depth, nor anything else in all creation, will be able to separate us from the love of God that is in Christ Jesus our Lord." **(Romans 8:38-39 NIV).***

ACTION: Before you do anything, pray to God to guide you

_____
_____

**Today is Feb 18th, Day #49 in year 2024,
There are 317 more days remaining in year 2024.**

PROCLAIM BEST BLESSINGS UNTO YOUR PROGENIES

SCRIPTURE: *"Joseph is like a vine that has lots of fruit. It grows near a well and its branches go over a wall. His enemies will be angry with him. They will attack him with arrows. But he will hold his own bow strongly. He will shoot his arrows well. The Mighty One of Jacob will give Joseph strength. God, who is Israel's Shepherd and Rock, will help him. The Almighty God, the God of your father, will help you and he will bless you. He will give you rain that comes from the sky above. He will give you springs of water from below the ground. He will cause you to have many descendants. That is how God will bless you. The blessings that I, your father, give to you are great! They are greater than any good things that the old mountains or hills can give to you. They are special blessings for you, Joseph, because you are the leader of your brothers." **(Genesis 49:22-26 EASY)***

PRAYER: Father, thank You for the wonderful children you have given us. They are Your heritage *(Psa 127:3)*. Please help each one of them to be successful in life, to serve You and to honor their parents *(Eph 6:2)*. In return, Father, teach us as parents, to love our children and constantly pray, prophesy and proclaim excellent and powerful blessings on our progenies (children) as did Jacob for his children, especially to Joseph

ACTION: Pray and proclaim blessings on your children every day.

_____

_____

Today is Feb 19th, Day #50 in year 2024,
There are 316 more days remaining in year 2024.

LISTED TO SERVE THE LORD?

SCRIPTURE: *"The grand total of all the Levites whom Moses, Aaron, and the leaders of Israel registered was 8,580. They were listed by families and households. These were the men between the ages of 30 and 50 who were qualified to do the work of serving and who carried the tent of meeting."* ***(Numbers 4:46-47 GW)***

PRAYER: Father, those of us who have given our lives to Jesus Christ and have decided to serve Him can be likened to the Levites who were qualified and enlisted to serve the Lord. By His grace we shall also reign with Him in God's kingdom. Oh Lord, please have mercy and draw by Your power those who have either refused to accept Your Salvation or are delaying the process thereby serving Satan whose goal is to lead such sinners into hell. Are you listed as saved serving the Lord and ready to reign with Him?. If not, do it today by accepting Him as Your Lord and Savior ***(John 3:16; Rom 10:9-13)***

ACTION: Encourage anyone you know who has not given his/her life to Jesus Christ to do so immediately to avoid their name from missing completely from the book of life

_____

_____

**Today is Feb 20th, Day #51 in year 2024,
There are 315 more days remaining in year 2024.**

MULTITUDE OF MERCIES FROM GOD OF MERCY

SCRIPTURE: *"Have mercy upon me, O God, According to Your lovingkindness; According to the multitude of Your tender mercies, Blot out my transgressions." (Psalm 51:1 NKJV)*

PRAYER: Father, thank You for Your lovingkindness and for being a God that is plenteous in mercy *(Psa 86:5,15; 103:8)*. Please Lord, have mercy on me and blot out my transgressions according to the multitude of Your tender mercies in Jesus' name, Amen

ACTION: Thank God for His mercy and grace that make salvation possible for those who will confess their sins and call on Jesus to forgive and save them.

_____

_____

**Today is Feb 21st, Day #52 in year 2024,
There are 314 more days remaining in year 2024.**

PRAISING JESUS FOR HIS GREAT POWER

SCRIPTURE: *"The disciples praised Jesus for his great power. Then they returned to Jerusalem, and they were all very happy. All the time they were in the temple, and they were praising God."* ***(Luke 24:52-53 EASY)***

PRAYER: Father, please let the praise of Jesus Christ continually be in my mouth as it was for King David ***(Psalm. 34:1)*** and Jesus' disciples ***(Lk 24:53)***. As I praise You, Lord Jesus, please empower me to do greater works in winning souls for You, healing the sick, casting out demons, prospering in all areas of my life, etc ***(John 14:12)***

ACTION: Provoke miracles to manifest by praising God as Paul and Silas did ***(Acts 16: 25-31)***

_____
_____

**Today is Feb 22nd, Day #53 in year 2024,
There are 313 more days remaining in year 2024.**

LED SAFELY BY THE LORD (II)

SCRIPTURE: *"And He led them on safely, so that they did not fear; But the sea overwhelmed their enemies." **(Psalms 78:53 NKJV)***

PRAYER: Father, in all my journeys in the year 2024 and beyond, please lead me safely in the path of righteousness and let me not fear. Let all my unrelenting enemies and destroyers drown in the sea in Jesus name.

ACTION: Pray to God to lead you in everything you do.

_____

_____

**Today is Feb 23rd, Day #54 in year 2024,
There are 312 more days remaining in year 2024.**

ERA OF POSITIVE ENLARGEMENT

SCRIPTURE: *"Sing, barren woman, you who never bore a child; burst into song, shout for joy, you who were never in labor; because more are the children of the desolate woman than of her who has a husband," says the Lord. "Enlarge the place of your tent, stretch your tent curtains wide, do not hold back; lengthen your cords, strengthen your stakes. For you will spread out to the right and to the left; your descendants will dispossess nations and settle in their desolate cities."* **(Isa 54:1-3 NIV)**

PRAYER: Father, Your word declares *"And out of them shall proceed thanksgiving and the voice of them that make merry: and I will multiply them, and they shall not be few; I will also glorify them, and they shall not be small"* **(Jeremiah 30:19)**. Almighty God, please let this season be our era of positive supernatural increases and enlargement. Let multitude of souls be won unto the Lord, the barren women to have many children as they want, the homeless to build their own houses and become landlords, transform all aspects of our economy from scarcity to surplus and give us leaders who will fear You and promote peace, unity, and rapid development in every nation in Jesus name.

ACTION: Give thanks and praise to God and claim His promise not to be small *(Jer. 30:19)*

**Today is Feb 24th, Day #55 in year 2024,
There are 311 more days remaining in year 2024.**

THE MENACES OF KING MANASSEH

SCRIPTURE: *"Manasseh was 12 years old when he began to rule, and he ruled for 55 years in Jerusalem., He did what the Lord considered evil by copying the disgusting things done by the nations that the Lord had forced out of the Israelites' way. He rebuilt the illegal places of worship that his father Hezekiah had torn down. He set up altars dedicated to other gods—the Baals—and made a pole dedicated to the goddess Asherah as King Ahab of Israel had done. Manasseh, like Ahab, worshiped and served the entire army of heaven... He burned his son as a sacrifice in the valley of Ben Hinnom, consulted fortunetellers, cast evil spells, practiced witchcraft, and appointed royal mediums and psychics. He did many things that made the Lord furious."* **(2 Chronicles 33:2-4, 6 GW)**

PRAYER: Father, in all nations, please supervise elections and the processes of choosing rulers such that only God-fearing, righteous, competent, and reputable persons will be chosen to rule Your people. Let all elections be conducted peacefully without rigging, war or shedding of blood. Please Lord, don't give us evil leaders like Manasseh who was one of the worst, wicked and wayward kings in Jerusalem whose tenure was full of menaces.

ACTION: Pray that, in all nations no wicked person will win in elections.

**Today is Feb 25th, Day #56 in year 2024,
There are 310 more days remaining in year 2024.**

GOD IS THE BEST GATHERER

SCRIPTURE: *"The Almighty Lord, who gathers the scattered people of Israel, declares, "I will gather still others besides those I have already gathered." (Isaiah 56:8 GW)*

PRAYER: Father, You are the best Gatherer and Your word declares *"...Whoever doesn't gather with me scatters." (Matthew 12:30 GW).*
Dear merciful Lord, our Maker and Savior, help us to partner with You in gathering and restoration of all scattered valuable resources (people, souls, finances, families, talents, times, marriages, etc).
Oh Lord, please rebuke the devourer and scatterer of our resources in Jesus' name.

ACTION: Pray to be a gatherer and not a scatterer of good things

_____
_____

**Today is Feb 26th, Day #57 in year 2024,
There are 309 more days remaining in year 2024.**

HELP FROM GOD THE MOST HIGH

SCRIPTURE: *"I will call to the Most High God to help me. He is the God who stands beside me. He will send help from heaven and he will save me. He will punish the people who attack me. Selah. God will show me his faithful love, and he will do what he has promised. My enemies are all round me, like hungry lions! I must lie down among wild animals, that want to eat me! They are men who use spears and arrows to bite like teeth. They use their tongues to hurt people, like sharp swords." (Psalms 57:2-4 EASY)*

PRAYER: Father, thank You for being my Defender, Deliverer, and my Present Help in times of troubles; Most High God, please send help to me from heaven, to defeat all my unrelenting enemies and safe me from their evil intentions in Jesus' name

ACTION: Pray that all the help you need will come timely from God

_____

_____

**Today is Feb 27th, Day #58 in year 2024,
There are 307 more days remaining in the year 2024.**

RECEIVING THE RIGHTEOUS MAN'S REWARD

SCRIPTURE: *"So that men will say, "Surely there is a reward for the righteous; Surely He is God who judges in the earth." **(Psalms 58:11 NKJV)***

PRAYER: Father, Your word declares, *"He who receives a prophet in the name of a prophet shall receive a prophet's reward. And he who receives a righteous man in the name of a righteous man shall receive a righteous man's reward."* **(Matthew 10:41 NKJV)**. Please Lord, give me the grace to do the needful to qualify for receiving both the prophet's and the righteous man's rewards in Jesus name.

ACTION: Prayerfully serve God with gladness and look up to Him for your rewards (Heb 11:6)

_____

_____

**Today is Feb 28th, Day #59 in year 2024,
There are 307 more days remaining in year 2024.**

SINGING TO GOD OF OUR STRENGTH

SCRIPTURE: *"But I will sing of thy power; yea, I will sing aloud of thy mercy in the morning: for thou hast been my defence and refuge in the day of my trouble. 17 Unto thee, O my strength, will I sing: for God is my defence, and the God of my mercy* **(Psalms 59:16-17 KJV).**

PRAYER: Father, Your word declares, *"I will sing unto the LORD as long as I live: I will sing praise to my God while I have my being"* **(Psalms 104:33).** Please Lord, keep me alive and let my mouth be perpetually filled with songs of praising You for Your strength, power, mercy and for being my refuge, defence, provider, etc, in Jesus name.

ACTION: Sing a joyful song unto God and praise Him seriously

_____

_____

**Today is Feb. 29th, Day #60 in year 2024,
There are 306 more days remaining in year 2024.**

SHOWCASED TO SHINE

SCRIPTURE: *"People of other nations will come to your light. Kings will come to see the light of a new day that shines on you."* ***(Isaiah 60:3 EASY)***

PRAYER: Father, please showcase me to shine as the light of the world to which people of other nations and kings will come to see the light of Your glory shinning on me in Jesus name.

ACTION: Pray that your light will never be dim nor go out

_____

_____

MARCH

Today is Mar.1st, Day #61 in year 2024,
There are 305 more days remaining in year 2024.

STAYING SAFE IN GOD'S SHELTER

SCRIPTURE: *"For You have been a shelter for me, A strong tower from the enemy. I will abide in Your tabernacle forever; I will trust in the shelter of Your wings. Selah"* **(Psalms 61:3-4 NKJV)**

PRAYER: Father, like You did for king David, please give me the grace to be passionately committed and inseparable from your Church (or tabernacle) so that I also will enjoy Your divine safety, shelter and protection against the wiles of the enemies *(Psa 27:4; Psa 69:9)*

ACTION: Let God be your shield always so that you can saved always

_____

_____

**Today is Mar. 2nd, Day #62 in year 2024,
There are 304 more days remaining in year 2024.**

SCATTERING ENEMIES' SCHEMES

SCRIPTURE: "You have heard their reproach, O Lord, All their schemes against me, The lips of my enemies And their whispering against me all the day." *(Lament. 3:61-62 NKJV)*

PRAYER: Father, Your word declares, *"When the enemy shall come in like a flood, the Spirit of the LORD shall lift up a standard against him"*. *(Isaiah 59:19b)*. Almighty God, please let Your Spirit lift up a standard against all my enemies to scatter all their evil schemes and machinations against me in Jesus' name *(Ex. 14:14)*

ACTION: Pray that your enemies' schemes against you will backfire as shame on them.

**Today is Mar. 3rd, Day #63 in year 2024,
There are 303 more days remaining in year 2024.**

LIFTING UP HANDS TO BLESS AND PRAISE THE LORD

SCRIPTURE: *"Thus I will bless You while I live; I will lift up my hands in Your name."* ***(Psalms 63:4 NKJV)***

PRAYER: Father, Your word declares, *"The dead cannot sing praises to the Lord, for they have gone into the silence of the grave."* ***(Psalms 115:17 NLT)***. Please Lord, give me the grace to pray and praise You more fervently, and like David, *"Let my prayer be set forth before thee as incense; and the lifting up of my hands as the evening sacrifice"* ***(Psalms 141:2)***

ACTION: Touch and call the name (e.g my mouth) all the parts of your body say each part belongs to Jesus (e.g 'my mouth, you belong to Jesus'). Praise God for every part of your body.

_____

_____

Today is Mar. 4th, Day #64 in year 2024,
There are 302 more days remaining in year 2024.

PROTECTION AGAINST ENEMIES' PLOTS

SCRIPTURE: *"Hide me from the secret plots of the wicked, From the rebellion of the workers of iniquity," **(Psalms 64:2 NKJV)***

PRAYER: Father, Your word declares, *"The Lord laughs at him [the wicked one—the one who oppresses the righteous], For He sees that his day [of defeat] is coming." **(Psalms 37:13 AMP)**.* Dear LORD, please deliver us from all wicked plotters and let them become shameful and disgraced laughing stocks as You defeat them woefully in Jesus name

ACTION: Pray that all the plots of the enemies against you will fail or backfire in Jesus' name.

**Today is Mar. 5th, Day #65 in year 2024,
There are 301 more days remaining in year 2024.**

LIVING VERY LONG

SCRIPTURE: *"Never again will there be a baby who only lives for a few days. Old men will continue to live a long life. People will live until they are 100 years old and they will still seem young. If anyone dies before he is 100 years old, people will think that God has cursed him."* **(Isaiah 65:20 EASY)**

PRAYER: Father, thank You for Your promise to satisfy us with long life *(Psa 91:15)* and to fulfill the number of our days *(Exo. 26:23)*. Dear Lord, please protect us from sudden and untimely death; by Your grace we decree like the Psalmist that we *"shall not die, but live, and declare the works of the LORD."* *(Psalms 118:17. KJV)*

ACTION: Pray that you will never die; after your long life here on earth, you will transition to eternity in the Kingdom of God *(John 11:26)*.

_____

_____

**Today is Mar.6th, Day #66 in year 2024,
There are 300 more days remaining in year 2024.**

ESCAPING FROM EXILE

SCRIPTURE: *"These are the people who returned to Jerusalem and the other towns in Judah. Nebuchadnezzar, king of Babylon, had brought them as prisoners to Babylon. Each person returned to his own town"; "666 descendants of Adonikam". "All together, 42,360 people returned to Jerusalem." (Ezra 2:1, 13, 64 EASY)*

PRAYER: Father, Your word declares,, *"If the Son therefore shall make you free, ye shall be free indeed" (John 8:36, KJV)*; please Lord, as You made a way of escape from exile for 666 descendants of Adonikam, please make a way of escape for us and our descendants from all forms of physical and spiritual exiles akin to that of Nebuchadnezzar in Jesus name

ACTION: Pray never to be a candidate for any type of exile, spiritual or physical

_____

_____

**Today is Mar. 7th, Day #67 in year 2024,
There are 299 more days remaining in year 2024.**

SEPARATING FROM THE SAVIOR?

SCRIPTURE: *"From that time, many of Jesus' disciples left him. They did not go with him any longer. Then Jesus asked the 12 apostles, 'Do you want to go away from me, too?'* **(John 6:66-67 EASY)**

PRAYER: Father, Your word declares,, *"....No man, having put his hand to the plough, and looking back, is fit for the kingdom of God* **(Luke 9:62)**; and that *"...they that forsake the LORD shall be consumed"* **(Isaiah 1:28, KJV)**; Dear Lord Jesus, please don't let me ever leave You; I decree that nothing shall be able to separate me from the love of God, which is in Christ Jesus my Lord, not tribulation, or distress, or persecution, or famine, or nakedness, or peril, or swords or death; nor life, nor angels, nor principalities, nor powers, nor things present, nor things to come, nor height, nor depth, nor any other creature, in Jesus name **(Romans 8:35-39)**

ACTION: Pray and determine never to abandon Jesus Christ as all His disciples did during His arrest **(Mark 14:43-50)**

_____

_____

**Today is Mar. 8th, Day #68 in year 2024,
There are 298 more days remaining in year 2024.**

SERVING GOD AS A FAMILY

SCRIPTURE: *"King David had chosen Asaph and his relatives to serve the Lord at the Covenant Box. They must do that each day, as the rules said that they should do. They included Obed-Edom and 68 men from his clan. Jeduthun's son, Obed-Edom and Hosah were guards at the entrance of the tent,* **(1 Chron. 16:37-38 EASY)**

PRAYER: Father, Your word declares, *"And if it seem evil unto you to serve the LORD, choose you this day whom ye will serve; whether the gods which your fathers served that were on the other side of the flood, or the gods of the Amorites, in whose land ye dwell: but as for me and my house, we will serve the LORD."* **(Joshua 24:15)**. Please Lord, let my family and I and our descendants serve You all the days of our lives in Jesus' name.

ACTION: Ensure your family has 'a vibrant family altar' with a schedule that allows all family members to regularly study God's word and pray together *(see Psa. 133:1-5)*.

_____

_____

Today is Mar. 9th, Day #69 in year 2024,
There are 297 more days remaining in year 2024.

CALLING FOR CHRIST'S INTIMACY AND RESCUE FROM ENEMIES

SCRIPTURE: *"Come very near to me and make me safe. Rescue me from my enemies." **(Psa.69:18 EASY)***

PRAYER: Father, thank You for Your faithfulness to Your promise to not leave me nor forsake me *(Heb13:5)*; Please Lord, by Your power please draw me to Yourself and rescue me from all my enemies in Jesus name

ACTION: Remain intimately connected with God who has promised to be with you in all circumstances and to fight for you *(Exo 14:14, John 15:5)*

_____

_____

Today is Mar. 10th, Day #70 in year 2024, There are 296 more days remaining in year 2024.

SERVANT OF GOD OR OF SATAN?

SCRIPTURE: *"Jesus replied, 'I have chosen the 12 of you. But one of you is a servant of Satan!'"* ***(John 6:70 EASY)***

PRAYER: Father, thank You for choosing me as one of Your servants based Your grace and my believe in, and acceptance of Jesus Christ as my Lord and Savior ***(John 1:12; 3:16)***; please don't let me turn aside to become servant of Satan as did Judas Iscariot ***(John 6:70-71; 1 Tim 5:15)***

ACTION: If you have not, give your life to Jesus Christ today and become His servant. You will spend eternity with Him in God's Kingdom ***(Dan. 7:18; John 14:1-3)***. Don't remain Satan's servant; for he and his servants are destined for lake of fire forever ***(Rev. 20:10, 15)***

Today is March 11th, Day #71 in year 2024.
There are 295 days remaining in 2024.

SHIELDED AGAINST SHAME

SCRIPTURE: *"In you, O Lord, do I put my trust and confidently take refuge; let me never be put to shame or confusion!" (Psa.71:1 AMPC).*

PRAYER: Father, thank You for being my Confidant, my Rock, my Fortress, my Deliverer; my God, my Strength, my Buckler, my Savior, and my High Tower *(Ps 18:2)*; please shield me from shame, sin, sickness, sorrows and all evils, IJN.

ACTION: Pray that nothing will change your glory to shame *(Hos 4:7)*

_____

_____

**Today is March 12th, day 72 in year 2024,
There are 294 more days remaining in year 2024.**

WORTH OF GOD'S WORD

SCRIPTURE: *The law from Your mouth is better to me than thousands of gold and silver pieces.* **(Psalm 119:72)**

PRAYER: Father, thank You for the great value of Your word which is beyond human description. First and foremost, Lord, You are an embodiment of Your word and by Your word the whole world and its dwellers including human beings were created **(John 1:1; Gen 1: 1-29)**. Furthermore, Your world declares; *".. the word of God is living and powerful, and sharper than any two-edged sword, piercing even to the division of soul and spirit, and of joints and marrow, and is a discerner of the thoughts and intents of the heart"* **(Heb 4:12)**. Please Lord, don't let Your word depart from my mouth, instead let Your word help me to avoid sinning **(Psa 119:11)**; heal me **(Psa 107:20)**; teach and instruct me the way to go **(Psa. 32:8)**, etc.

ACTION: Study and preach God's word to save souls **(2 Tim 2:15; 4:2)**

_____

_____

**Today is Mar. 13th, Day #73 in year 2024,
There are 293 more days remaining in year 2024.**

FASHIONED AND MADE BY GOD THE FATHER

SCRIPTURE: *"Your hands have made me and fashioned me; Give me understanding, that I may learn Your commandments." (Psalms 119:73 NKJV)*

PRAYER: Father thank You for making me in Your own image; *(Gen 1:26-28)*; please Lord give me the grace to understand and obey Your commandments. In particular, let me love You with all my heart, and with all my soul, and with all my mind, and with all my strength; let me also love my neighbor as myself in Jesus name *(Mark 12: 39-31)*. Oh Lord let me be fruitful, multiply, replenish the earth and have dominion in Jesus name

ACTION: Determine to love God by first keeping all His commandments for His word declares; "For this is the love of God, that we keep his commandments: and his commandments are not grievous. *(1John 5:3, KJV)*

_____

_____

**Today is Mar. 14th, Day #74 in year 2024,
There are 292 more days remaining in year 2024.**

SERVING GOD OF SAFETY

SCRIPTURE: *"God said, "I will keep you safe from your enemies. Then you can serve me and not be afraid."* **(Luke 1:74 EASY)**

PRAYER: Father, thank Your for Your word that says *"... safety is of the LORD"* **(Pro. 21:31b, KJV)**. As you continue to keep me safe from my enemies, please don't let me flinch in serving You with gladness in Jesus name

ACTION: Serve God assiduously and He will bless your bread and water and take sickness away from you in Jesus name *(Exo 23:25)*

_____
_____

**Today is Mar. 15th, Day #75 in year 2024,
There are 291 more days remaining in year 2024.**

ABRAHAMIC "ANOINTING"

SCRIPTURE: *"So Abram left Haran just like the Lord said, and Lot went with him. Abram was 75 years old when he left Haran."* ***(Gen 12: 4)***

PRAYER: Almighty God, thank you for the life of Abraham. Oh Lord, please give me the grace and endow me with virtues that enabled Abraham to walk before you and be perfect, to be faithful to you and to have his descendants blessed from generation to generation in Jesus name.

ACTION: Pray to always be a friend of God like Abraham ***(James 2:23)***

_____

_____

Today is Mar. 16th, Day #76 in year 2024, There are 290 more days remaining in year 2024

GOD OF GLORY

SCRIPTURE: *You are more glorious and excellent Than the mountains of prey (Psalm 76:4)*

PRAYER: Father, thank you for there is none like You; you are glorious in holiness, fearful in praises, doing wonders?" *(Isa.42:8)*. Furthermore, the heavens declare your glory… *(Psa 19:1)*. Please Lord manifests your glory and wonders in my life

ACTION: Pray that in God will be your salvation, your glory, your refuge and other blessings *(Psa 62:7)* and that whatever, you do will be done to the glory of God *(1 Cor10:31)*.

_____

_____

**Today is Mar. 17th, Day #77 in year 2024,
There are 289 more days remaining in year 2024**

FINDING SALVATION THROUGH FORGIVENESS

SCRIPTURE: *"You will tell his people how to find salvation through forgiveness of their sins." (Luke1:77 NLT)*

PRAYER: Father, Your word declares: *"He that believeth and is baptized shall be saved;" (Mark 16:16)*, and *"That if thou shalt confess with thy mouth the Lord Jesus, and shalt believe in thine heart that God hath raised him from the dead, thou shalt be saved" (Romans 10:9, KJV)*.
Oh Lord, please, let those yet unsaved know and follow the right way to receive salvation:
(a) acknowledge they have sinned *(Rom 3:23)*
(b) know the penalty for unconfessed sin is eternal death *(Rom 6:23)*
(c) Confess their sins and ask for forgiveness *(Rom 10:9)*
(d) By faith, accept the grace, forgiveness and salvation offered by Jesus Christ and ask Him to be their Lord and Savior henceforth

ACTION: If you have been saved, give thanks to Jesus Christ for your salvation. Then Intercede for those unsaved to find salvation through forgiveness of their sins by Jesus Christ. Share this ministration with any unsaved person you know.

_____

_____

Today is Mar. 18th, Day #78 in year 2024, There are 288 more days remaining in year 2024.

MERCY INDUCED HEAVENLY MORNING LIGHT

SCRIPTURE: *"Because of God's tender mercy, the morning light from heaven is about to break upon us,"* **(Luke1:78 NLT)**

PRAYER: Father, Your word declares: *"Surely goodness and mercy shall follow me all the days of my life: and I will dwell in the house of the LORD forever"*, **(Psalm 23:6, KJV)**; Oh Lord, the Dayspring from on high, please visit me with Your mercy and let Your tender and heavenly morning light break forth on me every day in Jesus name.

ACTION: Emulate the psalmist and praise God as in **Psa. 59:16**: *"But I will sing of Your power; Yes, I will sing aloud of Your mercy in the morning; For You have been my defense And refuge in the day of my trouble."*

_____

_____

**Today is Mar. 19th, Day #79 in year 2024,
There are 287 more days remaining in year 2024**

POWER OF GOD CAN LIBRATE PRISONERS

SCRIPTURE: *"Listen to the prisoners who are in pain! They are calling out for help. Use your great power to make them free, before their enemies kill them."* ***(Psalms 79:11 EASY)***

PRAYER: Father, thank You for Your great power by which You set the Israelites free from the Egyptian captivity *(Exo 12)*; as well as other prisoners like Joseph, Peter, Paul and Silas, etc, that You set free from various prisons *(Gen. 39; Acts 22; 16:25-35)*. Almighty God, by Your great power please liberate all prisoners from all forms of pain and imprisonment (physical, spiritual. sickness, bareness, persistent failure, etc)

ACTION: Pray/sing aloud about the power and tender mercy of God daily and command darkness to vanish from your life. Read *Psa 59:16*

Today is Mar. 20th, Day #80 in year 2024,
There are 286 more days remaining in year 2024.

BACKSLIDERS MUST COME BACK

SCRIPTURE: *"God, turn us to come back to you. Look at us with a smile on your face! Then we will be safe."* ***(Psalms 80:3 EASY)***

PRAYER: Father, Your word declares, "Now the just shall live by faith: but if any man draw back, my soul shall have no pleasure in him. ***(Heb. 10:38)***; Dear Lord, please don't let us ever draw back from You. Let all backsliders repent and be reconciled with You in Jesus name.

ACTION: Pray that God will use you as a change agent to draw backsliders back to HIM by Your great power please liberate all prisoners from all forms of pain and imprisonment (physical, spiritual. sickness, bareness, persistent failure, etc)

_____

_____

Today is Mar. 21st, Day #81 in year 2024, There are 285 more days remaining in year 2024.

FED BY GOD WITH THE BEST FOOD

SCRIPTURE: *"But I would feed you, my people, with the best wheat. I would give you plenty of honey from the rock, for you to eat and be full."* ***(Psalms 81:16 EASY)***

PRAYER: Father, please give me the grace to be willing and obedient to You so that I can eat the best of the land in plenty and be satisfied, praising You ***(Isa 1:19; Joel; 2:26)***

ACTION: Let us give thanks to God who has been meeting our need for food and other things. Pray to be in the position to feed those who are hungry and needy.

_____

_____

Today is Mar. 22nd, Day #82 in year 2024,
There are 284 more days remaining in the year 2024

GOD'S CHILDREN CALLED "gods"

SCRIPTURE: *"I have said, Ye are gods; and all of you are children of the most High"* ***(Psa 82:6.)***

PRAYER: Father, thank You for creating me in Your own image ***(Gen 1:27)***, and giving me the privilege to be your representative or ambassador called 'god' as well as saving my soul and redeeming me to be your child and a joint heir with Jesus Christ your begotten son ***(Rom 8:17)***.

ACTION: To qualify to be called 'god' the child of the most High God, you must have given your life to Jesus Christ as Your Lord and savior. If you haven't done so, do it today.

_____

_____

Today is Mar. 23rd, Day #83 of in year 2024,
There are 283 more days remaining in year 2024.

CONSPIRACY AGAINST GOD AND HIS PEOPLE

SCRIPTURE: *"For they have consulted together with one consent; They form a confederacy against You:"* ***(Psalms 83:5 NKJV)***

PRAYER: Father, arise, frustrate, confuse, wage war against and destroy all who have adamantly conspired to attack You and Your people in Jesus name.

ACTION: Pray to God to change your conspirators to collaborators

_____
_____

Today is Mar. 24th, Day #84 of in year 2024, There are 282 more days remaining in year 2024

REWARDS FROM GOD FOR DOING RIGHT

SCRIPTURE: *"The Lord God is like a sun and a shield for his people. He is kind to his people, and he gives glory to them. To those who do what is right, he gives every good thing that they need." (Psalms 84:11 EASY)*

PRAYER: Father, thank You for You are the source of all good and perfect gifts *(James 1:17)*; please give us the grace to always do what is right in Your sight and to have all our needs met according to Your riches in glory by Christ Jesus.

ACTION: Trust and thank God daily to be your Shield and Supplier of all your needs

_____

_____

**Today is Mar. 25th, Day #85 in year 2024,
There are 281 more days remaining in year 2024**

PITS DUG BY THE WICKED PROUD

SCRIPTURE: *"The proud have dug pits for me, Which is not according to Your law." **(Psalms 119:85 NKJV)***

PRAYER: Father, Your word declares, *"An ungodly man digs up evil, And it is on his lips like a burning fire." **(Prov. 16:27 NKJV)*** Almighty God, please let the pits dug for me by the proud and wicked enemies become their final place of unrest in accordance to Your word that, *"Whoso diggeth a pit shall fall therein: and he that rolleth a stone, it will return upon him"* ***(Proverbs 26:27)***

ACTION: Let's watch and pray never to fall into any physical and spiritual pits dug for us by the proud

_____

_____

Today is Mar. 26th, Day #86 in year 2024,
There are 280 more days remaining in year 2024

AMAZING AND NUMEROUS ARE GOD'S ATTRIBUTES (1)

SCRIPTURE: *"But You, O Lord, are a God full of compassion, and gracious, Longsuffering and abundant in mercy and truth."* ***(Psalms 86:15 NKJV)***

PRAYER: Father, thank You for Your wonderful attributes some of which You proclaimed to Moses in ***Exo 34:6-7***. Please give us the grace to emulate You in been compassionate, loving, gracious, full of mercy, long suffering, forgiving, etc, in Jesus name

ACTION: Holiness is the bedrock of God's attributes. No wonder His word says, *"..Be ye holy; for I am holy."* ***(1 Peter 1:16)***. Let us prayerfully pursue holiness *"..,without which no man shall see the Lord"* ***(Hebrews 12:14)***

_____

_____

Today is Mar. 27th, Day #87 in year 2024, There are 279 more days remaining in year 2024

DIVINE INCREASE

SCRIPTURE: *"Though your beginning was small, Yet your latter end would increase abundantly."* ***(Job 8:7 NKJV)***

PRAYER: Father, Your word declares, *"The LORD shall increase you more and more, you and your children.'* ***(Psalms 115:14)***. Dear Lord, please bless me and my family and give us divine and valuable increases in Jesus name

ACTION: Give thanks to God for that which He has done already in terms of 'daily benefits' ***(Psa 68:19)***

_____

_____

Today is Mar. 28th, Day #88 in year 2024, There are 278 more days remaining in year 2024.

PRAYERS RECEIVED AND ANSWERED

SCRIPTURE: *"Let my prayer come before You; Incline Your ear to my cry"* ***(Psalms 88:2 NKJV)***

PRAYER: Father, please whenever I pray to You, please hear me and answer me according to Your promise : "He shall call upon Me, and I will answer him; I will be with him in trouble; I will deliver him and honor him ***(Psalms 91:15 NKJV)***.

ACTION: Let us remember to testify on answered prayers ***(Rev 12:11)***

_____

_____

**Today is Mar. 29th, Day #89 in year 2024,
There are 277 more days remaining in year 2024**

MAKER AND OWNER OF HEAVEN AND EARTH: GOD THE MIGHTY

SCRIPTURE: *"The heavens are yours. The earth is also yours. You made the world and everything in it."* **(Psa. 89:11 GW)**

PRAYER: Father, Your word declares, *"The earth is the Lord's, and all its fullness, The world and those who dwell therein....."* **(Psa.24:1-2 NKJV)**; please Lord, let Your will and agenda prevail in every part of the world so that we Your people will dwell in peace to praise and worship You freely in Jesus name

ACTION: By prayer, claim your location for Godly ownership based on ***Joshua 1:3***: *"Every place that the sole of your foot shall tread upon, that have I given unto you, as I said unto Moses"*

_____
_____

**Today is Mar. 30th, Day #90 in year 2024,
There are 276 more days remaining in year 2024**

GETTING BLESSINGS ON OUR WORK FROM GOD

SCRIPTURE: *"And let the beauty of the Lord our God be upon us, And establish the work of our hands for us; Yes, establish the work of our hands."* ***(Psalms 90:17 NKJV)***

PRAYER: Father, please give me the grace to diligently obey Your voice and observe carefully all Your commandments and let me attract Your blessings as stated in ***Deut. 28: 3-6***: *"Blessed shall be the fruit of your body, the produce of your ground and the increase of your herds, the increase of your cattle and the offspring of your flocks. "Blessed shall be your basket and your kneading bowl. "Blessed shall you be when you come in, and blessed shall you be when you go out."* in Jesus name

ACTION: Pray to God to bless all your efforts in all you do

_____

_____

**Today is Mar. 31st, Day #91 in year 2024,
There are 275 more days remaining in year 2024**

SAFETY FOR THE GODLY

SCRIPTURE: *"I will say of the Lord, "He is my refuge and my fortress; My God, in Him I will trust."* ***(Psalms 91:2 NKJV)***

PRAYER: Father, as one You have redeemed, freed from sins ***(Psa 107:2; Rom 6:22)***, my safety is in You ***(Pro 21:31, Deut 33:12)***; Please let no weapon fashioned against me and all mine prosper in Jesus name ***(Isa 54:17; Psa 18:2)***

ACTION: Give thanks to God for successful and safe completion of the month of March 2024

_____

_____

APRIL

**Today is April 1st, Day #92 in year 2024,
There are 274 more days remaining in year 2024**

FRUITFUL AND FLOURISHING

SCRIPTURE: *"Those who are planted in the house of the Lord Shall flourish in the courts of our God. They shall still bear fruit in old age; They shall be fresh and flourishing," (Psa.92:13-14 NKJV)*

PRAYER: Father, please give me the grace to remain planted in Your house so that I can be fruitful, fresh and flourishing perpetually in Jesus's name.

ACTION: Give thanks to God for the new month of APRIL. Pray for divine protection, peace and provisions throughout the new month. Your life shall be full of Godly blessings in Jesus name

_____

_____

**Today is April 2nd, Day #93 in year 2024,
There are 273 more Remaining in year 2024**

RULERSHIP BY THE REDEEMER

SCRIPTURE: "But the Lord rules as King high above everything! He rules over the powerful waves of the sea, with all their great noise!" *(Psalms 93:4 EASY)*

PRAYER: Father, thank You for being a greatly surpassing ruler: the Highest, the Holiest, the Strongest, the Most Merciful, King of kings and the Lord of lords, please subdue every evil force that wants to rule my life

ACTION: Command every power contending with God in your life to vamoose by fire in Jesus name

_____

_____

Today is April 3rd, Day #94 in year 2024,
There are 272 more days remaining in year 2024

RULERSHIP BY THE REDEEMER

SCRIPTURE: *"But the Lord rules as King high above everything! He rules over the powerful waves of the sea, with all their great noise!"* ***(Psalms 93:4 EASY)***

PRAYER: Father, thank You for being a greatly surpassing ruler: the Highest, the Holiest, the Strongest, the Most Merciful, King of kings and the Lord of lords, please subdue every evil force that wants to rule my life

ACTION: Command every power contending with God in your life to vamoose by fire in Jesus name

_____

_____

Today is April 4th Day #95 in year 2024,
There are 271 more days remaining in year 2024.

PUNISHMENT FOR PROUD PEOPLE

SCRIPTURE: *"Judge of all people on the earth, do something! Punish proud people as they deserve!"* **(Psalms 94:2 EASY)**

PRAYER: Father thank You for You are a righteous Judge by whom *"..actions are weighed"* **(1 Sam 3:2)**; please have mercy on all proud people and let them repent in order to avoid Your punishment as in **Malachi 4:1**: *""For behold, the day is coming, Burning like an oven, And all the proud, yes, all who do wickedly will be stubble. And the day which is coming shall burn them up,...."* **(Malachi 4:1 NKJV)**

ACTION: Is any one close to you proud or showing the sign thereof?; pray for him/her to cast out the spirit of pride and minister to the person as you are led,

_____

_____

**Today is April 5th Day #96 in year 2024,
There are 270 more days remaining in the year 2024**

HARDEN NOT YOUR HEART

SCRIPTURE: *"The Lord says, "Don't harden your hearts as Israel did at Meribah, as they did at Massah in the wilderness." **(Psalms 95:8 NLT)***

PRAYER: Father, please foil every attempt of Satan to make me harden my heart against You. Please Lord, don't let me be a victim of a habitual hardness, and long custom in sinning; and any other type of negative hardness of heart

ACTION: Pray against and cancel the spirit of hardness of heart in all children and grandchildren in Jesus name

_____
_____

**Today is April 6th Day #97 in year 2024,
There are 269 more days remaining in year 2024.**

FORESAKING THE FOOLISH

SCRIPTURE: *"Forsake foolishness and live, And go in the way of understanding"* ***(Pro 9:6)***

PRAYER: Father, Your word declares, *"The fool has said in his heart, "There is no God." They are corrupt, They have done abominable works, There is none who does good"* ***(Psa 14:1)***; Oh Lord, please don't let me be yoked with the foolish so that I can live, follow the way of understanding, and not suffer harm ***(Pro 13:20)***.

ACTION: To avoid being a grief to your parents and God, don't be a fool and don't get hooked to a fool ***(Pro17:24)***

_____

_____

**Today is April 7th Day #98 in year 2024,
There are 268 more days remaining in year 2024.**

'FOR OUR GOD IS A CONSUMING FIRE'

SCRIPTURE: *"The Lord is king! Let the earth rejoice! Let the farthest coastlands be glad. Dark clouds surround him. Righteousness and justice are the foundation of his throne. Fire spreads ahead of him and burns up all his foes." (Psa.97:1-3 NLT)*

PRAYER: Father, Your word declares, *"You will capture all your enemies. Your strong right hand will seize all who hate you. You will throw them in a flaming furnace when you appear. The Lord will consume them in his anger; fire will devour them." (Psalms 21:8-9 NLT)*. Oh LORD, please let all those who have refused to give their lives to Jesus Christ do so immediately before it's too late and they are thrown into the lake of fire *(Rev 20:15)*.

ACTION: Thank God for this day and pray that the Consuming fire will destroy every attempt of Satan to tamper with your day today

_____

_____

**Today is April 8th Day #99 in year 2024,
There are 267 more days remaining in year 2024.**

SING TO THE LORD PRAISES AND NEW SONGS

SCRIPTURE: *"Sing your praise to the Lord with the harp, with the harp and melodious song,"* **(Psalms 98:5 NLT)**

PRAYER: Father, Your word declares, *"Praise ye the LORD. Sing unto the LORD a new song, and his praise in the congregation of saints"* **(Psa. 149:1 KJV)**; Please LORD, give me the grace to bless You at all times and let Your praise continually be in my mouth in Jesus name *(Psa 34:1)*

ACTION: Thank God for this day and sing unto Him as many praise songs as you can

_____

_____

**Today is April 9th Day #100 in year 2024,
There are 266 more days remaining in year 2024**

APPEARANCE OF GOD TO ABRAHAM

SCRIPTURE: *"When Abram was 99 years old, the Lord appeared to him. The Lord said, 'I am God Almighty. In all your life, obey me and do nothing wrong." **(Genesis 17:1 EASY)***

PRAYER: Lord Jesus, thank You because, as God Your Father appeared to Abraham, You also appeared to Your followers and disciples several times after Your resurrection *(Mark 26:1-11, John 20:24-29; Luke 24:33-34)*. As we celebrate Your resurrection this season, we are grateful for Your love, compassion and the sacrifice You made to redeem us. for us in terms of paying the penalty for our sins with Your life. Please give us more divine revelations about Yourself and Your words.

ACTION: Pray to God to give you faith like Abraham, help you to live holy and to reveal Himself more to you by His grace.

_____

_____

**Today is April 10th Day #101 in year 2024,
There are 265 more days remaining in year 2024**

POWER TO PREVAIL

SCRIPTURE: *"Five of you will run after 100 of them. And 100 of you will run after 1,000 enemies. You will kill all your enemies."* **(Lev. 26:8 EASY)**

PRAYER: Father, You word declares that, *"One man of you shall chase a thousand: for the LORD your God, he it is that fighteth for you, as he hath promised you. "* **(Joshua 23:10)**. Dear LORD, please fight for me and let me supernaturally prevail over all my enemies in Jesus name

ACTION: Let God be Your weapon of warfare *(2 Cor 10:4)*

_____

_____

**Today is April 11th Day #102 in year 2024,
There are 264 more days remaining in year 2024**

LIVING A BLAMELESS LIFE

SCRIPTURE: *"I will be careful to live a blameless life—when will you come to help me? I will lead a life of integrity in my own home." (Psalms 101:2, NLT.)*

PRAYER: Father, Your word declares *"Blessed are those whose ways are blameless, who walk according to the law of the Lord." (Psa. 119:1 NIV).* Dear Lord, please give me the enablement to walk before You blameless as did Abraham who You blessed and his descendants abundantly *(Psa 15)*. With Your help oh Lord, I will live a life of integrity in Jesus name

ACTION: Prayfully and determine to be holy and blameless *(1 Pet 1:16, Luke 1:37)*

_____

_____

**Today is April 12th, Day #103 in year 2024,
There are 263 more days remaining in year 2024**

GOD ENDURES FOREVER AND HIS NAME IS REMEMBERED TO ALL GENERATIONS

SCRIPTURE: *"But You, O Lord, shall endure forever, And the remembrance of Your name to all generations." **(Psa. 102:12)***

PRAYER: Father, thank You for Your enduring nature, loving kindness, mercy and the fact that, 'from everlasting to everlasting, Thou art God' ***(Psa 90:2b)***. Please Lord, let nothing stop me from serving You to the end and from reigning with You in eternity in Your kingdom in Jesus name.

ACTION: Remember always that *"Jesus Christ is the same yesterday, today, and forever." **(Hebrews 13:8 NKJV)***

_____

_____

Today is April 13th Day #104 in year 2024,
There are 262 more days remaining in year 2024

BLESSING GOD AND REMEMBERING ALL HIS BENEFITS

SCRIPTURE: *"Bless the Lord, O my soul, And forget not all His benefits:" **(Psalms 103:2 NKJV)***

PRAYER: Father, thank You for Your enduring nature, loving kindness, mercy and the fact that, 'from everlasting to everlasting, Thou art God' *(Psa 90:2b)*. Please Lord, let nothing stop me from serving You to the end and from reigning with You in eternity in Your kingdom in Jesus name.

ACTION: Remember always that *"Jesus Christ is the same yesterday, today, and forever." **(Hebrews 13:8 NKJV)***

_____

_____

**Today is April 14th Day #105 in year 2024,
There are 261 more days remaining in year 2024**

WONDERFUL AND MANIFOLD ARE GOD'S WORKS

SCRIPTURE: *"O Lord, how manifold are Your works! In wisdom You have made them all. The earth is full of Your possession"* ***(Psalms 104:24 NKJV)***

PRAYER: Father, as suggested by the Psalmist, I praise You for Your *"..goodness and wonderful works to the children of men"* ***(Psa 107: 8, 15, 21, 31)***. Dear Lord, please continue to manifest wonderful and manifold works in all areas of my life. Furthermore, please Lord, endow me with wisdom, strength, and all that I need to do greater exploits that will glorify You in Jesus name ***(Dan 11:32)***

ACTION: Remember that with God all things are possible ***(Mark 10:27b)***

_____

_____

Today is April 15th Day #106 in year 2024,
There are 260 more days remaining in year 2024

DANGER OF FORESAKING GOD THE FATHER (Judges 10: 6-7)

SCRIPTURE: *"Then the children of Israel again did evil in the sight of the Lord, and served the Baals and the Ashtoreths, the gods of Syria, the gods of Sidon, the gods of Moab, the gods of the people of Ammon, and the gods of the Philistines; and they forsook the Lord and did not serve Him. 7 So the anger of the Lord was hot against Israel; and He sold them into the hands of the Philistines and into the hands of the people of Ammon"*

PRAYER: Father, please don't let me forsake you under any circumstance as the consequences for so doing are grievous as Your word declares, *"The Lord will send on you cursing, confusion, and rebuke in all that you set your hand to do, until you are destroyed and until you perish quickly, because of the wickedness of your doings in which you have forsaken Me* **(Deut 28:20.)**

ACTION: Always remember God's word says, *"..without me you can do nothing"* **(John 15:5)** and determine never to leave God

Today is April 16th Day #107 in year 2024, There are 259 more days remaining in year 2024

REWARD FOR ACTING JUSTLY AND DOING RIGHT

SCRIPTURE: *"Blessed are those who act justly, who always do what is right." **(Psa. 106:3 NIV)***

PRAYER: Father, according to ***Psalm 119:112***, please give me the grace to *"incline my heart to perform Your statutes Forever, even to the end"* and to always act justly and do what is right so that I may enjoy perpetual blessings from You in Jesus name.

ACTION: Determine to always live by faith, a virtue typical of the just ***(Heb 10:38)***

**Today is April 17th Day #108 in year 2024,
There are 258 more days remaining in year 2024**

STOP THE SUFFERING

SCRIPTURE: *"I have suffered much; preserve my life, Lord, according to your word."* ***(Psalms 119:107 NIV)***

PRAYER: Father, Your word declares, *"Thou shalt also decree a thing, and it shall be established unto thee: and the light shall shine upon thy ways"* ***(Job 22:28)***; I decree that enough is enough and all forms of sufferings must come to an end now in my life in Jesus name

ACTION: Where necessary and inevitable suffer for/with Christ so you can reign with Him ***(2 Tim 2:12)***

_____
_____

Today is April 18th Day #109 in year 2024, There are 257 more days remaining in year 2024

PEOPLE OF GOD RESCUED BY HIS POWER

SCRIPTURE: *"Now rescue your beloved people. Answer and save us by your power."* ***(Psalms 108:6 NLT)***

PRAYER: Father, thank You for the grace we have to be among Your beloved servants, please continue to hear us, answer us and, by Your power save us from our enemies in Jesus name

ACTION: Pray to God to rescue Christians who are facing persecutions in different parts of the world

_____

_____

Today is April 19th, Day #110 in year 2024, There are 256 more days remaining in year 2024

ATTACKING THE ATTACKERS

SCRIPTURE: *"Appoint someone evil to oppose my enemy; let an accuser stand at his right hand." **(Psalms 109:6 NIV)***

PRAYER: Father, by Your grace let all my enemies repent and back off from me; otherwise, if they refuse and are adamant to harm me, please send evil attackers to destroy them before they destroy me in Jesus name

ACTION: Plead the blood of Jesus on yourself and claim the scripture in ***Gal 6:17***

_____

_____

Today is April 20th, Day #111 in year 2024,
There are 255 more days remaining in year 2024

PART NOT FROM GOD'S PRECEPTS

SCRIPTURE: *"The wicked have set a snare for me, but I have not strayed from your precepts." **(Psalms 119:110 NIV)***

PRAYER: Father, please don't let me ever depart from Your precepts for Your word declares, *"I will instruct thee and teach thee in the way which thou shalt go: I will guide thee with mine eye." **(Psalms 32:8)**.* Oh Lord, let the snare of the wicked set for me backfire in Jesus name

ACTION: Plead the blood of Jesus on yourself and claim the scripture in Pro 26:27

_____

_____

Today is April 21st, Day #112 in year 2024,
There are 254 more days remaining in year 2024

GREAT ATTRIBUTES OF DEEDS OF GOD (1)

SCRIPTURE: *"Great are the works of the Lord; they are pondered by all who delight in them. Glorious and majestic are his deeds, and his righteousness endures forever." (Psalms 111:2-3 NIV)*

PRAYER: Father, thank You for Your word declares *"And God saw every thing that he had made, and, behold, it was very good…"(Gen.1:31)*. Please Lord, bless me and let good, great, glorious, majestic, wonderful, and enduring works manifest in my life in Jesus name.

ACTION: Plead the blood of Jesus on yourself and claim the scripture in *Psa 90:17*

_____

_____

Today is April 22nd, Day #113 in year 2024,
There are 253 more days remaining in year 2024

UNENDING REWARDS FOR OBEYING GOD'S LAWS

SCRIPTURE: *"I have decided to obey your laws. They offer a reward that never ends." **(Psalms 119:112 GW)***

PRAYER: Father, thank You for You are the One who works in me both to will and to do Your good pleasure *(Phil 2:13 NKJV)*; Lord, please give me the grace to keep Your law continually, Forever and ever *(Psa.119:44 NKJV)*, and to obtain rewards from You that will never end in Jesus name

ACTION: Plead the blood of Jesus on yourself and claim the scripture in **Deut 28:1-14.**

_____

_____

**Today is April 23rd, Day #114 in year 2024,
There are 252 more days remaining in year 2024**

PROMOTER OF THE POOR AND WEAK PEOPLE

SCRIPTURE: *"He lifts poor people out of the dirt. And he lifts up weak people from the ashes."* ***(Psalms 113:7 EASY)***

PRAYER: Father, thank You for You are the ultimate promoter as no person can promote like You ***(Psa 75:6)***; as You raised David and many others from the lowest stair to the very highest step of honour and opulence, please have mercy and do the same for those who are poor in spirit (lack salvation by Jesus Christ)and/or poor physically (barren, hungry, homeless, destitute etc)

ACTION: Plead the blood of Jesus on yourself and claim the scripture in ***3 John verse 2***

_____

_____

**Today is April 24th, Day #115 in year 2024,
There are 251 more days remaining in year 2024**

MIRACLE OF TURNING ROCK TO WATER

SCRIPTURE: *"He turns a rock into a pool filled with water and turns flint into a spring flowing with water."* **(Psalms 114:8 GW)**

PRAYER: Father, Your word declares. *"For with God nothing shall be impossible."(Luke 1:37)*. Please turn every scarce (but needful) resource in my life to surplus as You did for the Israelites in the wilderness when they lacked water and, through Moses, You turned a rock into a pool filled with water *(Num 20:11)*

ACTION: Plead the blood of Jesus on yourself and claim the scripture **Psalms 107:35**: *"He turneth the wilderness into a standing water, and dry ground into watersprings."*

Today is April 25th, Day #116 in year 2024, There are 250 more days remaining in year 2024

ELIMINATE DETRACTORS AND EVILDOERS

SCRIPTURE: *"Depart from me, you evildoers, For I will keep the commandments of my God!"* ***(Psalms 119:115 NKJV)***.

PRAYER: Father, Your word declares *"Be ye not unequally yoked together with unbelievers: for what fellowship hath righteousness with unrighteousness? and what communion hath light with darkness?"* ***(2 Cor. 6:14 KJV)***. Dear LORD, please chase all evil doers and detractors away from me and give me the grace to keep all Your commandments in Jesus name

ACTION: Plead the blood of Jesus on yourself and claim the scripture ***Psalms 118:17***

_____

_____

Today is April 26th, Day #117 in year 2024,
There are 249 more days remaining in year 2024

ATTRIBUTES OF GOD II

SCRIPTURE: *"Gracious is the Lord, and righteous; Yes, our God is merciful." **(Psalms 116:5 NKJV)***

PRAYER: Father thank You for your many and wonderful attributes. You are full of grace by which You saved me *(John 1:14; Eph 2:8)*; Oh LORD our God, Your right hand is full of righteousness *(Psa 48:10)* and You are righteous in all Your work *(Dan 9:14)*. Furthermore, Lord, You are *"..plenteous in mercy and truth" **(Psa. 86:15)*** with which You *"..hath clothed me with the garments of salvation, and covered me with the robe of righteousness"**(Isaiah 61:10)***.

ACTION: Pray that wherever you go today, God's presence and wonderful attributes will accompany you in Jesus name

**Today is April 27th, Day #118 in year 2024,
There are 248 more days remaining in year 2024**

SAFE AND SECURED IN GOD'S HAND

SCRIPTURE: *"Hold me up, and I shall be safe, And I shall observe Your statutes continually."* ***(Psalms 119:117 NKJV)***.

PRAYER: Father Your word declares *"The eternal God is thy refuge, and underneath are the everlasting arms: and he shall thrust out the enemy from before thee; and shall say, Destroy them."* ***(Deut.33:27)***. Dear Lord, please empower me to obey Your statutes continually and to remain safe in Your arms in Jesus name.

ACTION: Plead the blood of Jesus on yourself and claim God's promise in ***Isa 54:17***

**Today is April 28th, Day #119 in year 2024,
There are 247 more days remaining in year 2024**

PRAYING FOR SALVATION AND PROSPERITY

SCRIPTURE: *"Save now, I pray, O Lord; O Lord, I pray, send now prosperity." **(Psa. 118:25 NKJV)***

PRAYER: Father Your word declares *"...seek first the kingdom of God and His righteousness, and all these things shall be added to you." **(Matthew 6:33 NKJV)***. Dear Lord, thank You for the salvation of my soul; please save others through me. Let me continue to obey and serve You and let me spend my days in prosperity, and my years in pleasures in Jesus name ***(Job 36:11; Psa 30:6)***

ACTION: Plead the blood of Jesus on yourself and claim God's promise in ***Psa. 34:10b.***

_____

_____

Today is April 29th, Day #120 in year 2024, There are 246 more days remaining in year 2024

PRAYING FOR DIVINE UNDERSTANDING

SCRIPTURE: *"I am Your servant; Give me understanding, That I may know Your testimonies." **(Psalms 119:125 NKJV)***.

PRAYER: Father Your word declares *"Wisdom is the principal thing; therefore, get wisdom: and with all thy getting get understanding." **(Pro 4:7)***. To know Your word better and do greater exploits, please Lord give me divine understanding as You did for: Bezaleel and Aholiab ***(Exo 36:1; 35:31)***; Solomon ***(1 King 4:29)***; Daniel ***(Dan. 1:17)*** in Jesus name.

ACTION: Plead the blood of Jesus on yourself and claim the scripture: *"But there is a spirit in man, And the breath of the Almighty gives him understanding." **(Job 32:8 NKJV)***.

_____

_____

Today is April 30th, Day #121 in year 2024,
There are 245 more days remaining in year 2024

DELIVERANCE FROM LIARS AND THE DECEITFUL

SCRIPTURE: *"Rescue me, O Lord, from liars and from all deceitful people." **(Psalms 120:2 NLT)***

PRAYER: Father, as prayed by the psalmist please *"Rescue me and deliver me from the hand of foreigners, Whose mouth speaks lying words, And whose right hand is a right hand of falsehood"*. **(Psa. 144:11 NKJV)**

ACTION: Plead the blood of Jesus on yourself and pray and claim **Psalms 120:2**: *"Deliver my soul, O LORD, from lying lips, and from a deceitful tongue."*

_____

_____

MAY

**Today is May 1st, Day #122 in year 2024,
There are 244 more days remaining in year 2024.**

HELP FROM THE LORD

SCRIPTURE: *"My help comes from the Lord, the Maker of heaven and earth." **(Psalms 121:2 NIV)***

PRAYER: Father, we thank You that You are *"... our refuge and strength, a very present help in trouble" **(Psa. 46:1)***. Oh ever faithful God, please continue to help us out of the hands of all our enemies and their troubles and afflictions; in the performance of our duty unto You, in the supply of Your grace, and many blessings unto us and in all areas of our needs according to ***Phil 4:19***, in fulfilling our destinies and in making it into Your kingdom in Jesus name.

ACTION: Plead the blood of Jesus on yourself and claim ***Isaiah 41:13***

_____

_____

**Today is May 2nd, Day #123 in year 2024,
There are 243 more days remaining in year 2024.**

PRAYING FOR JERUSALEM'S PEACE

SCRIPTURE: *"Pray for the peace of Jerusalem: "May those who love you be secure." **(Psa. 122:6 NIV)***

PRAYER: Father, Your word declares, *"Blessed be the LORD out of Zion, which dwelleth at Jerusalem. Praise ye the LORD." **(Psalms 135:21)**.* Please Lord: Let there be peace in Jerusalem.
Let Jerusalem remain a holy city. Let people of Jerusalem Praise You always. Let Jerusalem overcome her enemies
Please let the people of Jerusalem accept You as Their Lord and Savior *(Jer 4:14)*.

ACTION: In this month of GRACE let's prayerfully claim *2 Cor 9:8*

_____

_____

Today is May 3rd, Day #124 in year 2024.
There are 242 days remaining in the year 2024.

LIFTING UP EYES TO THE LORD

SCRIPTURE: *"I lift up my eyes to you, to you who sit enthroned in heaven."* ***(Psalms 123:1 NIV)***

PRAYER: Father, Your word declares *"looking unto Jesus, the author and finisher of our faith,.."* ***(Heb 12:2 NKJV).*** Dear Lord, please let me keep my gaze on You at all times for Your unfailing mercies, divine deliverance, and guaranteed victories over the enemies for You are my refuge and strength, A Very Present help in trouble ***(Psa. 46:1)***

ACTION: Prayerfully Claim the scripture ***Psa 84:1***

Today is May 4th, Day #125 in year 2024.
There are 241 days remaining in the year 2024.

PREVENTED BY GOD FROM BEING A PREY

SCRIPTURE: *"Blessed be the Lord, Who has not given us as prey to their teeth." **(Psa. 124:6 NKJV)***

PRAYER: Father, Your word declares *"If it had not been the Lord who was on our side, When men rose up against us, Then they would have swallowed us alive...." **(Psa. 124:2-3 NKJV)***. Thank You Lord for delivering us from various enemies, seen and unseen. Dear Lord, please prevent us from being preys to Satan and his agents who are seeking who to devour *(1 Peter 5:8)*

ACTION: Prayerfully Claim the scripture *Exo 14:14*

_____
_____

Today is May 5th, Day #126 in year 2024.
There are 240 days remaining in the year 2024.

PRAYER FOR THE GOOD AND UPRIGH AT HEART PEOPLE

SCRIPTURE: *"Do good, O Lord, to those who are good, And to those who are upright in their hearts."* ***(Psalms 125:4 NKJV)***

PRAYER: Father, Your word declares l, *"....whatsoever a man soweth, that shall he also reap"* ***(Gal. 6:7, KJV)***; Oh Lord, by Your grace please let me be among the people who are/will be good and are/ will be upright at heart to whom You will do good in Jesus name

ACTION: Prayerfully Claim the scripture ***Psalm 23:6***

Today is May 6th, Day #127 in year 2024.
There are 239 days remaining in year 2024

GLADNESS RESULTING FROM GREAT THINGS DONE FOR US BY GOD

SCRIPTURE: *"Then was our mouth filled with laughter, and our tongue with singing: then said they among the heathen, The LORD hath done great things for them. The LORD hath done great things for us; whereof we are glad."* ***(Psa 126: 2-3)***.

PRAYER: Father, thank You for the great work of salvation and other things You have done that has brought joy and gladness into our lives. Please Lord do more of great things for us in our health, homes, families, finances, careers, ministries, etc. Please, don't let our gladness turn into sorrow in Jesus' name.

ACTION: As the redeemed of the Lord, prayerfully claim the scripture in ***Isaiah 51:11***

_____

_____

**Today is May 7th, Day #128 in year 2024.
There are 238 days remaining in the year 2024.**

CHILDREN ARE A GIFT AND REWARD FROM GOD

SCRIPTURE: *"Children are a gift from the Lord; they are a reward from him." (Psalms 127:3 NLT).*

PRAYER: Father, thank You for the children You have given us who belong to You just as we their biological parents. Please help us to Train up our children in Your ways so that they will know You and serve You without departing from You *(Proverbs 22:6)*. Together with our children please protect us, provide for us, perfect all that concern us and let us all make it into Your kingdom to reign with Jesus till eternity in Jesus' name.

ACTION: As the redeemed of the Lord Prayerfully Claim the scripture in *Isaiah 51:1*

_____

_____

**Today is May 8th, Day #129 in year 2024.
There are 237 days remaining in year 2024**

BLESSED AND PROSPERING FROM SELF LABOR

SCRIPTURE: *"You will eat the fruit of your labor; blessings and prosperity will be yours."* ***(Psalms 128:2 NIV)***

PRAYER: Father, Your word declares *"They shall not build, and another inhabit; they shall not plant, and another eat: for as the days of a tree are the days of my people, and mine elect shall long enjoy the work of their hands"* ***(Isaiah 62:22)***. Dear Lord, please bless and prosper the work of my hands; by Your grace I shall not labor for someone else to reap the blessings in Jesus name

ACTION: As one blessed by the Lord claim the scripture ***Isaiah 65:23***

_____

_____

Today is May 9th, Day #130 in year 2024.
There are 236 days remaining in the year 2024.

RIGHTEOUS GOD HAS CUT OFF THE WICKED'S ROPES

SCRIPTURE: *"The Lord is righteous. He has cut me loose from the ropes that wicked people tied around me."* ***(Psalms 129:4 GW)***

PRAYER: Father, Your word declares *"No weapon that is formed against thee shall prosper; and every tongue that shall rise against thee in judgment thou shalt condemn. This is the heritage of the servants of the LORD, and their righteousness is of me, saith the LORD." **(Isaiah 54:17 KJV)***. Please Lord, let every rope prepared by the wicked ones to hurt me catch fire in Jesus name

ACTION: Pray for yourself and family using ***Psalm 141:9***

Today is May 10th, Day #131 in year 2024.
There are 235 days remaining in the year 2024.

FEARING GOD FOR HIS FORGIVENESS?

SCRIPTURE: *"If You, Lord, should mark iniquities, O Lord, who could stand? But there is forgiveness with You, That You may be feared." **(Psalms 130:3-4 NKJV)**.*

PRAYER: Father, we thank You for Your readiness to always forgive us our sins, for Your word declares, *"If we confess our sins, He is faithful and just to forgive us our sins and to cleanse us from all unrighteousness."**(I John 1:9 NKJV)**.* Please Lord, don't let us continue in sins and expect grace to continue *(Rom 6:1)*; Instead let us be wise enough to have reverential fear for You so as not to sin against You but to abstain from all iniquities in Jesus' name.

ACTION: Prayerfully determine not to let sin have dominion over you in Jesus name *(Rom 6:14)*.

_____

_____

Today is May 11th, Day #132 in year 2024.
There are 234 days remaining in year 2024

LONGING AND PANTING FOR COMMANDS OF THE LORD

SCRIPTURE: *"I open my mouth and pant because I long for your commands." **(Psalms 119:131)**.*

PRAYER: Father, Your word declares *"Like newborn infants, desire the pure milk of the word...."*, ***(1 Pet.2:2)***. Please Lord give me the grace to have a longing for Your word so as to study and meditate on it every day and to observe and obey all Your commandments in Jesus name

ACTION: Prayerfully do what is said in ***II Timothy 2:15***

**Today is May 12th, Day #133 in year 2024.
There are 233 days remaining in year 2024**

PRAYER FOR GOD'S PRIESTS AND FAITHFUL PEOPLE

SCRIPTURE: *"May your priests be clothed with righteousness, and may your faithful people shout for joy." (Psalms 132:9)*

PRAYER: Lord Jesus thank You for Your love and generosity that led You to make us kings and priests unto God Your Father… *(Rev. 1:6 KJV)*
Father, as Your priests, please clothe us with garments of righteousness and as Your faithful people let us always have reasons to rejoice in You.

ACTION: Prayerfully do what is said in *Philippians 4:4, NKJV*

_____

_____

Today is May 13th, Day #134 in year 2024.
There are 232 days remaining in the year 2024.

DIRECTED BY GOD'S WORD TO DOMINATE SINS.

SCRIPTURE: *"Direct my steps by Your word, And let no iniquity have dominion over me."* ***(Psalms 119:133 NKJV)***

PRAYER: Father, please let Your word be *"..a lamp to my feet And a light to my path." **(Psa.119:105 NKJV)*** to guide me in walking circumspectly, not as fools but as wise, redeeming the time, because the days are evil." ***(Eph. 5:15-16 NKJV).*** Dear Lord, let me also hide Your word always in my heart so as not to sin against You. ***(Psa. 119:11 NKJV)***

ACTION: Prayerfully do what is said in ***(Joshua 1:8, NKJV)***

_____

_____

Today is May 14th, Day #135 in year 2024.
There are 231 days remaining in the year 2024.

LIFTING UP HANDS TO BLESS AND PRAISE THE LORD.

SCRIPTURE: *"Lift up your hands in the sanctuary, And bless the Lord"* **(Psalms 134:2 NKJV).**

PRAYER: Father, Your word declares *"Let us lift up our hearts and our hands to God in heaven"* **(Lam. 3:41)** and *"Therefore, I want the men in every place to pray, lifting up holy hands without anger or argument"* **(1 Tim. 2:8)**
Almighty God, as part of honoring, praying, praising and worshipping You help us to lift our holy hands to You without anger or argument.
Father, please strengthen and anoint the same hands I lift up to You such that they become healing hands, carriers of good and perfect gifts, hands that do greater exploits and achieve success and victory in all endeavors in Jesus name.

ACTION: Pray God to train Your hands to do what is said in *(Psa 18:34 & Psa 144:1)*

_____

_____

**Today is May 15th, Day #136 in year 2024.
There are 230 days remaining in year 2024**

GREATNESS OF GOD

SCRIPTURE: *"For I know that the Lord is great, And our Lord is above all gods. Whatever the Lord pleases He does, In heaven and in earth, In the seas and in all deep places." (Psa.135:5-6 NKJV)*.

PRAYER: Father, Your word declares *"The LORD is great and is highly praised; his greatness is unsearchable"*. *(Psa. 145:3)*. Thank You Lord for it is further said of You that. *"He does great and unsearchable things, wonders without number" (Job 5:9, 10)*. Please Lord, continue to demonstrate Your greatness in all areas of my life as You promised Abraham and his descendants *(Gen 22:1-3)*

ACTION: Pray for more anointing to do greater works *(John 14:12)*

_____

_____

Today is May 16th, Day #137 in year 2024. There are 229 days remaining in year 2024

GRIEVED GREATLY BY THE RAMPANT DISOBEDIENCE TO GOD'S LAWS?

SCRIPTURE: *"Rivers of waters run down mine eyes, Because they keep not thy law." **(Psa. 119:136)***

PRAYER: Father, help us not to be nonchalant when we see Your law despised, disobeyed and Your name dishonored and not given the glory which is due unto You. Instead, lord lead and guide us how to pray and counsel such wicked people to respect God's word and follow God's injunction given to the Israelites: *"Thy word have I hid in mine heart, That I might not sin against thee." **(Psalm 119:11 KJV)***

ACTION: Pray to emulate the Psalmist per ***Psalm 119:11***

_____

_____

Today is May 17th, Day #138 in year 2024. There are 228 days remaining in year 2024

FRUITFUL OR FRUITLESS?

SCRIPTURE: *"Then said he unto the dresser of his vineyard, Behold, these three years I come seeking fruit on this fig tree, and find none: cut it down; why cumbereth it the ground?" (Luke 13:7 KJV).*

PRAYER: Father, thank You for Jesus Christ, the true vine *(John 15:1)*. By Your grace and my faith in Jesus Christ that made my salvation possible, I am one of His 'branches'. Oh Lord, please let me continue to abide in You as a branch so that I can be more fruitful in all areas of my life and also get all my requests answered in Jesus name *(John 15:4-5;7)*

ACTION: Pray for those who are not yet 'branches' of Jesus Christ, not abiding in Him and /or are fruitless, that they will soon do the needful and avoid been thrown into fire *(John 15:6)*.

_____

_____

**Today is May 18th, Day #139 in year 2024.
There are 227 days remaining in year 2024**

PRAISING GOD WHOLEHEARTEDLY

SCRIPTURE: *"I will praise You with my whole heart; Before the gods I will sing praises to You."* ***(Psalms 138:1 NKJV).***

PRAYER: Father, Your word declares *"Great is the Lord, and greatly to be praised; And His greatness is unsearchable **(Psalms 145:3 NKJV).***
Dear Lord, for Your mercies and innumerable blessings upon me and my families I have nothing to give You but to say thank You Lord. Please Lord don't let Your praise depart from my mouth

ACTION: Let us determine to praise God at all times, for all things

_____

_____

Today is May 19th, Day #140 in year 2024.
There are 226 days remaining in the year 2024.

RIGHTEOUS VERSUS WICKED PEOPLE

SCRIPTURE: *"The light of righteous people beams brightly, but the lamp of wicked people will be snuffed out." (Pro.13:9 GW)*

PRAYER: Father, thank You for Your Son Jesus Christ who has made it possible for me to *"..become the righteousness of God in Him." (II Cor. 5:21 NKJV)*. Please, Lord let me arise and shine and let my path be *"...like the shining sun, that shines ever brighter unto the perfect day." (Pro. 4:18 NKJV)*. Lord, please let my glory and success last very long. By Your power oh Lord, let darkness swallow and snuff out all evil and wicked people who are determined to hurt me

ACTION: Prayerfully claim *Isa 60:1*

_____

_____

Today is May 20th, Day #141 in year 2024.
There are 225 days remaining in the year 2024.

DELIVERANCE FROM WICKED AND VIOLENT PROPLE

SCRIPTURE: *"Keep me, O Lord, from the hands of the wicked; Preserve me from violent men, Who have purposed to make my steps stumble."* ***(Psa. 140:4 NKJV)***

PRAYER: Father, please be to me what You were to the Psalmist who said *"The Lord is my rock and my fortress and my Savior, my God, my rock in whom I take refuge, my shield, and the strength of my salvation, my stronghold."* ***(Psalms 18:2 GW)***
Almighty God, please fight for me and consume by fire all my unrelenting violent and wicked enemies who have purposed to make me stumble.

ACTION: Prayerfully claim what is said in ***Deut. 28:7***.

_____
_____

Today is May 21st, Day #142 in the year 2024.
There are 224 days remaining in the year 2024.

ANTITHESIS BETWEEN WISE AND FOOLISH WOMAN

SCRIPTURE: *"The wise woman builds her house, But the foolish pulls it down with her hands." **(Proverbs 14:1 NKJV)***

PRAYER: Father, in all our families please let our wives and mothers of our children know Your and be endowed with wisdom for building their homes and their communities as did Leah and Rachael of Israel *(Ruth 4:11)*. Lord, please help our women to be prudent, provident and good trainers of children in Godly ways. Please Lord don't let our women be like the foolish woman who pulls down her house by being wasteful, idle, lavish, proud, quarrelsome and complaining perpetually. Dear Lord thank You for giving me a wife who is wise, loving, caring and builder of home

ACTION: Pray for peaceful and glorious services today everywhere people will gather to worship the Almighty God

**Today is May 22nd, Day #143 in year 2024.
There are 223 days remaining in the year 2024**

PEOPLE CHOSEN BY GOD FOR POSSESSION

SCRIPTURE: *"You have been set apart as holy to the Lord your God, and he has chosen you from all the nations of the earth to be his own special treasure." **(Deuteronomy 14:2 NLT)***

PRAYER: Father, thank You for choosing me as one of Your own saved, set apart, holy, peculiar, special and treasured people **(Deut. 14:2; Isaiah 43:1)**. Please Lord, give me the grace to continue to serve You as a dedicated and diligent servant, worshipper and soul winner who will enjoy peculiar blessings and privileges and benefits such as freedom from debts, sicknesses, poverty, etc.

ACTION: Prayerfully claim the scripture *Isaiah 43:4*

**Today is May 23rd, Day #144 in year 2024.
There are 222 days remaining in the year 2024.**

PLEADING FOR GOD'S HELP AND PROTECTION

SCRIPTURE: *"In Your mercy cut off my enemies And destroy all those who afflict my soul; For I am Your servant." (Psalms 143:12 NKJV)*

PRAYER: Father, by Your creation, redemption, grace, mercy and call to serve You, please fight for me, cut off my enemies and destroy all those who afflict my soul as You promised in **Deut 3:22; 20:4**; and as You did for Moses, Daniel, David, Elisha, Moses, Jehoshaphat etc. in Jesus name.

ACTION: Prayerfully claim the scripture, Isaiah **Exo 24:14**

_____

_____

Today is May 24th, Day #145 in year 2024.
There are 221 days remaining in year the 2024.

GOD: THE SKILL GIVER

SCRIPTURE: *". Blessed be the Lord my Rock, Who trains my hands for war, And my fingers for battle"* **(Psalms 144:1 NKJV)**

PRAYER: Father, Your word declares *"Wisdom is better than weapons of war…"* **(Eccl. 9:18)** and that *"Wisdom is the principal thing; Therefore get wisdom, ….."***(Prov4:7 NKJV)*. Lord, please give me wisdom, skills and trained hands for success and victory in all my endeavors as You did for David who defeated Goliath *(1Sam 17)*; and for Jehoshaphat and Judah who successfully defeated armies of 3 nations *(II Chron 20)*.

ACTION: Prayerfully claim the scriptures *Isaiah 54:17* and *2Cor 10:4*

_____

_____

Today is May 25th, Day #146 in year 2024.
There are 220 days remaining in the year 2024.

DIVINE INVESTMENT

SCRIPTURE: This perfume could have been sold for a high price, and the money could have been given to the poor. *"So they said some very unkind things to her." (Mark 14:5 GW)*

PRAYER: Father, Your word declares *"Cast thy bread upon the waters: for thou shalt find it after many days." (Ecc. 11:1)*, and that, *"……..Assuredly, I say to you, there is no one who has left house or parents or brothers or wife or children, for the sake of the kingdom of God, who shall not receive many times more in this present time, and in the age to come eternal life." (Luke 18:29-30 NKJV).* Dear Lord, in the remaining 220 days of this year and the rest of my life, please give me the grace to always make divine investments by giving generously (sowing seeds toward kingdom agenda and the propagation of the Gospel of Jesus Christ) that will attract dividends akin to that of the woman with alabaster box of costly oil *(Mark 24)*, Abraham *(Gen 22)*, the widow of Zarepath *(1 Kings 17: 8-17)*, the boy who sacrificed his 'lunch' which Jesus blessed and used to feed more than 10 thousand people with 12 baskets leftover *(Mark 6)*.

ACTION: Prayerfully obey the injunction as in *Luke 6:38*

**Today is May 26th, Day #147 in year 2024.
There are 219 days remaining in year 2024**

LIVING AS UNTO THE LORD

SCRIPTURE: *"He that regardeth the day, regardeth it unto the Lord; and he that regardeth not the day, to the Lord he doth not regard it. He that eateth, eateth to the Lord, for he giveth God thanks; and he that eateth not, to the Lord he eateth not, and giveth God thanks." **(Romans 14:6 KJV)***

PRAYER: Father, You word declares *"…without me ye can do nothing." **(John 15:5 KJV)**.*
Thank You for all you have enabled me to do so far this year. Oh Lord, for the remaining 219 days of this year and for the rest of my life let me live and do things not unto self but 'in the name of the Lord Jesus'*(Col 3:17)* and *'to the glory of God' (1 Cor 10:31)*

ACTION: Let us pray that God will bless us in all the works of our hand *(Deut 2:7)*

_____

_____

**Today is May 27th, Day #148 in year 2024.
There are 218 days remaining in the year 2024.**

FORSAKING THE FOOL

SCRIPTURE: *"Leave the presence of a [shortsighted] fool, For you will not find knowledge or hear godly wisdom from his lips."* **(Proverbs 14:7 AMP)**

PRAYER: Father, Your word declares *"The fool hath said in his heart, There is no God. They are corrupt, they have done abominable works, there is none that doeth good"* **(Psa 14:1; 53:3)**. Almighty God, please don't let me be associated (and unequally yoked) with fools and doers of abominable who will influence me negatively and cause me to sin against You.

ACTION: Prayerfully follow the injunction that says: *"Abstain from all appearance of evil."* **(1 Thessalonians 5:22 KJV).**

Today is May 28th, Day #149 in year 2024.
There are 217 days remaining in year 2024.

FOLLOWING GOD WHOLEHEARTEDLY

SCRIPTURE: *"but my brothers who went with me frightened the people from entering the Promised Land. For my part, I wholeheartedly followed the Lord my God." **(Josh 14:8 NLT)***.

PRAYER: Father, Your word declares *"..but the righteous are bold as a lion" **(Pro. 28:1b)***; Oh Lord, with respect to faith and doing Your biddings let fear be far from me so that I can follow You boldly and wholeheartedly, remain healthy and strong and, akin to Caleb, receive promised rewards that exceed bountiful in Jesus name

ACTION: Let us pray to emulate Caleb and follow God fully *(Josh.14:14)*

_____

_____

**Today is May 29th, Day #150 in year 2024.
There are 216 days remaining in year 2024.**

HAVING THE FAITH FOR HEALING

SCRIPTURE: *"He listened to Paul as he was speaking. Paul looked directly at him, saw that he had faith to be healed and called out, "Stand up on your feet!" At that, the man jumped up and began to walk." (Acts 14:9-10 NIV).*

PRAYER: Father, Your word declares, *"...If ye have faith as a grain of mustard seed, ye shall say unto this mountain, Remove hence to yonder place; and it shall remove; and nothing shall be impossible unto you" (Matthew 17:20, KJV).* Oh Lord please increase my faith such that any 'mountain' (or problem) I tell to move must move unfailingly as it happened for the man crippled from the womb whose faith Paul saw and healed him *(Acts 14:8-10)*

ACTION: Let us pray to have faith to please God always *(Heb 11:6)* and faith to heal and be healed

_____

_____

Today is May 30th, Day #151 in year 2024.
There are 215 days remaining in the year 2024.

GREAT PRAISE TO A GREAT GOD

SCRIPTURE: *"Praise him for his mighty acts: praise him according to his excellent greatness." **(Psalms 150:2, KJV)***

PRAYER: Father, praise and thanks to You for Your mighty and innumerable acts including the creation of all things out of nothing; the sustaining of all beings and the redemption of man by Jesus Christ and His wonderful works of miracles performed on earth. Oh Most Excellent and Great God, please give me the grace and power to praise You without ceasing for all You have done and will do for me, my family and all readers of the postings on this platform. *(Psa 34:1)*

ACTION: Let us prayerfully praise God and claim the rewards for so doing as indicated in *Psa. 67:3-7*

_____

_____

Today is May 31st, Day #152 in year 2024.
There are 214 days remaining in year 2024.

GIVING UP PERSONAL RESOURCES FOR GOD'S USE

SCRIPTURE: *"David built houses for himself in the City of David; and he prepared a place for the ark of God and pitched a tent for it." **(I Chronicles 15:1 NKJV)***

PRAYER: Father, Your word declares *"Cast thy bread upon the waters: for thou shalt find it after many days"* ***(Eccl. 11:1)*** and that, *"...whatsoever a man soweth, that shall he also reap." **(Gal. 6:7)***. Please Lord give us heart of gratitude and appreciation so as to give generously (out our talents, time and treasures received from You) to support Your works as did David; the Shunammite woman who hosted Elisha *(2 Kings 4:8-37);* the Widow of Zarephath who fed Elijah *(2 kings 17:7-16)*, and early Christians *(Acts 2:42-47)*, etc

ACTION: Read Acts 20:35 and remember that no one can out give God

_____

_____

JUNE

**Today is June 1st, Day #153 in year 2024.
There are 213 days remaining in year 2024.**

LONGEVITY OF GOD'S LAWS

SCRIPTURE: *"I have known from my earliest days that your laws will last forever." **(Psa. 119:152 NLT)***

PRAYER: Father, Your word declares *"..For ever, O LORD, thy word is settled in heaven"* ***(Psalms 119:89)*** and that *"Heaven and earth will pass away, but My words will by no means pass away."**(Matt 24:35)***
Oh Lord, please let nothing delay, derail or debar the manifestation of all your spoken words and promises concerning my life, such: I shall live and not die,
No weapon fashioned against me shall prosper, I shall be head and not tail, I shall not lack any good thing, I shall prosper and be in health, No weapon fashioned against me shall prosper, I shall eat and be satisfied, etc

ACTION: Prayerfully claim the scripture ***2 Cor.a1:20***

_____
_____

Today is June 2nd, Day #154 in year 2024.
There are 212 days remaining in year 2024.

DELIVERANCE FROM DISTRESSES

SCRIPTURE: *"Consider mine affliction and deliver me: for I do not forget thy law.* **(Psalms 119:153, KJV)**

PRAYER: Father, concerning the Israelites Your word declares *"They wandered in the wilderness in a desolate way; They found no city to dwell in. Hungry and thirsty, Their soul fainted in them. Then they cried out to the Lord in their trouble, And He delivered them out of their distresses." **(Psa 107:4-6 NKJV)**.* Oh Lord, as You did for the Israelites and for David several times **(Psa 18:6; 118:5; 220:1)** as we cry to You today, please deliver us from all troubles and distresses (spiritual, physical, health, financial, job-related, etc)

ACTION: Let no problem destabilize you, by faith claim *Psa 107:6* and cry to God to deliver you

_____

_____

**Today is June 3rd, Day #155 in year 2024.
There are 211 days remaining in year 2024.**

DESTROYING PHARAOH BY DROWNING

SCRIPTURE: *"Pharaoh's chariots and his host hath he cast into the sea: his chosen captains also are drowned in the Red sea. -Exodus 15:4*

PRAYER: Father, let every 'Pharaoh' planning to truncate my destiny by troubling me with afflictions, hard labor and enslavement drown and perish in the Red Sea in Jesus name

ACTION: Prayerfully claim the scripture in *John 8:36*.

Today is June 4th, Day #156 in year 2024.
There are 210 days remaining in year 2024.

CRITERIA FOR REMAINING UNMOVABLE IN JESUS CHRIST

SCRIPTURE: *"He who does not put out his money at usury, Nor does he take a bribe against the innocent. He who does these things shall never be moved."* ***Psalms 15:5 NKJV***

PRAYER: Father, Your word declares: *"As you therefore have received Christ Jesus the Lord, so walk in Him, rooted and built up in Him and established in the faith, as you have been taught, abounding in it with thanksgiving." **(Col. 2:6-7 NKJV).***
Dear, Lord, please don't let me do anything that will separate me from You, for in You I live, move and have my being ***(Acts 17:28a)***

ACTION: Prayerfully claim the scripture ***Rom 8:39***

_____

_____

**Today is June 5th, Day #157 in the year 2024.
There are 209 days remaining in the year 2024.**

REVIVED PER DIVINE REGULATIONS

SCRIPTURE: *"Lord, how great is your mercy; let me be revived by following your regulations."* **Psalms 119:156 NLT**

PRAYER: Father, please revive me with Your great mercy, love and compassion that will quicken me to rejoice again, love You the more, serve You more diligently and hold fast to all Your promises which are yea and Amen *(2 Cor 1:20)*

ACTION: Prayerfully claim the scripture, Rom 85:6: *"Wilt thou not revive us again: that thy people may rejoice in thee?"* *-Psalms 85:6*

_____
_____

Today is June 6th, Day #158 in year 2024.
There are 208 days remaining in year 2024.

OPENING HEART AND HAND TO HELP THE POOR

SCRIPTURE: *"If there is among you a poor man of your brethren, within any of the gates in your land which the Lord your God is giving you, you shall not harden your heart nor shut your hand from your poor brother,"* ***(Deuteronomy 15:7 NKJV)***

PRAYER: Father, Your word declares, *"Blessed is he who considers the poor; The Lord will deliver him in time of trouble."* ***(Psa 41:1 NKJV)*** and that, *"He who has pity on the poor lends to the Lord, And He will pay back what he has given."*** (Proverbs 19:17 NKJV)***
Dear Lord God, please give me a heart of compassion so as to give generously to the poor instead of having closed heart and hand toward them.

ACTION: Give unto the poor and the needy as generous as you can and claim the scripture *Acts 20:35*

_____

_____

**Today is June 7th, Day #159 in year 2024.
There are 207 days remaining in year 2024.**

ACTING LIKE KING ASA

SCRIPTURE: *"When Asa heard the prophet Oded's words of prophecy, he was encouraged and put away the detestable idols from all of Judah, Benjamin, and the cities he had captured in the mountains of Ephraim. He also repaired the Lord's altar in front of the Lord's entrance hall." (2 Chronicles 15:8 GW)*

PRAYER: Father, Your word declares, *"Thou shalt have no other gods before me" (Exo 20:3)* and that You will honor those who honor You *(1 Sam 2:20)*. Dear Lord, as individuals and as rulers give us the courage to emulate king Asa who the Bible says *"did what was good and right in the eyes of the Lord his God" (2 Chron. 14:2)*. Furthermore Asa instituted religious reform leading to the removal of the male shrine prostitutes, cutting down of Asherah poles, etc *(1 Kings 15:12–13; 2 Chron. 14:3, 16)*. Asa also commanded his people to follow the Lord *(2 Chron 14:4)*. Almighty and everlasting God, please let our hearts, like that of Asa, be fully committed to the Lord all our life *(2 Chronicles 15:17)*.

ACTION: Let's not give room to any form of idol. When tempted, declare to Satan, the scripture in *Luke 4: 8*.

_____

_____

Today is June 8th, Day #160 in year 2024.
There are 206 days remaining in year 2024.

DON'T DISCRIMINATE

SCRIPTURE: *"God doesn't discriminate between Jewish and non-Jewish people. He has cleansed non-Jewish people through faith as he has cleansed us Jews." (Acts 15:9 GW)*

PRAYER: Father, thank You for making us in Your own image. As You do not show partiality *(Rom 2:11, NKJV)*; please help us not to discriminate or practice partiality so as not to sin by violating Your second most important commandment: *"....Love your neighbor as yourself...."(Mark 12:28-31, NIV)*.

ACTION: Let us pray fervently for eradication of discrimination in our society as 'Discrimination is a clog in the wheel of development and progress.

_____

_____

Today is June 9th, Day #161 in the year 2024.
There are 205 days remaining in the year 2024.

INFALLIBILITY OF GOD'S WORD

SCRIPTURE: *"All your words are true; all your righteous laws are eternal."* ***(Psalms 119:160 NIV)***

PRAYER: Father, Your word declares that, *".. the word of God came, and the scripture cannot be broken"* ***(John 10:35)*** and that, *"All scripture is given by inspiration of God..."* ***(2Tim 3:16)***.
Dear Lord, by the power in Your word ***(Heb 4:12)***, it's infallibility and inerrancy, please inspire me and direct all my affairs such that I will be successful and not stumble in Jesus name

ACTION: Let's do like the Psalmist: *"I will delight myself in thy statutes: I will not forget thy word"* ***(Psalms 119:16)***

Today is June 10th, Day #162 in year 2024.
There are 204 days remaining in year 2024.

PROTECTION BY GOD, THE TRUSTED HIDING PLACE

SCRIPTURE: *"Protect me, O God, because I take refuge in you." **(Psalms 16:1 GW)***

PRAYER: Father, Your word declares that, "I will say of the LORD, He is my refuge and my fortress: my God; in him will I trust" (Psalms 91:2). My Father, my Father, my trust is in You, please protect me, my family and all people connected with me in accordance with Your word that says, *"Thou wilt keep him in perfect peace, whose mind is stayed on thee: because he trusteth in thee"* **(Isa 26:3, KJV)**.

ACTION: Prayerfully claim the scripture in Isaiah 46:4

_____

_____

Today is June 11th, Day #163 in year 2024.
There are 203 days remaining in year 2024.

GETTING AHEAD OF GOD?

SCRIPTURE: *"So Sarai said to Abram, "See now, the Lord has restrained me from bearing children. Please, go in to my maid; perhaps I shall obtain children by her." And Abram heeded the voice of Sarai."* **(Gen.16:2 NKJV)**

PRAYER: Father, Your word declares, *"For the vision is yet for an appointed time, but at the end it shall speak, and not lie: though it tarry, wait for it; because it will surely come, it will not tarry"* **(Habakkuk 2:3)**. Dear Lord, please give us the grace to wait patiently for the fulfillment of Your promises to us AT YOUR OWN ORDAINED TIME. Oh Lord, please don't let us attempt to outrun your schedule as Sarah appear to have done when she persuaded Abraham to have a child with Hagar **(Gen 16)**

ACTION: Pray against delays

_____

_____

Today is June 12th, Day #164 in year 2024.
There are 202 days remaining in year 2024.

LOVING GOD'S LAWS AND HATING LIES

SCRIPTURE: *"I hate and abhor lying: but thy law do I love"* ***(Psalms 119:163)***

PRAYER: Father Your word declares, *"You who love the Lord, hate evil! ..."* ***(Psalms 97:10 NKJV)***. Oh Lord please let me continue to love You and Your laws and to hate lying, sins and all forms of evil in Jesus name.

ACTION: Pray for a lifestyle that embraces the scriptures ***Rom 6:14*** and ***Joshua 23:14***

_____

_____

Today is June 13th, Day #165 in year 2024. There are 201 days remaining in year 2024

GOD'S CREATIONS ARE GOOD

SCRIPTURE: *"The LORD hath made all things for himself: yea, even the wicked for the day of evil"* **(Proverbs 16:4)**

PRAYER: Father Your word declares, *"And God saw every thing that he had made, and, behold, it was very good....."* *(Gen.1:31)*. Oh Lord, let all things You have made give You honor and glory. Let those who on their own turned from good to wickedness repent and be saved to avoid Your wrath and condemnation on judgement day

ACTION: Let us give thanks to God for creating us good in His own image

Today is June 14th, Day #166 in year 2024.
There are 200 days remaining in year 2024.

PRIDE CARRIES PUNISHMENTS

SCRIPTURE: *"Every one that is proud in heart is an abomination to the LORD: though hand join in hand, he shall not be unpunished"* **(Pro. 16:5)**

PRAYER: Father Your word declares that *"Pride goeth before destruction, and an haughty spirit before a fall."* **(Proverbs 16:18)**.
The Bible says Satan was cast out of heaven because of pride *(Isa 14:12-15)*. Dear Lord, please deliver us from the kind of pride that You hate *(Pro 18:13)* and the one that stems from self-righteousness or conceit that leads to sin and dangerous punishments. In place of pride help us to cultivate humility at all times in Jesus name *(James 4:6)*

ACTION: Prayerfully choose humility and abhor pride

_____

_____

**Today is June 15th, Day #167 in year 2024.
There are 199 days remaining in year 2024.**

GOD'S PLEASANT GIFTS AND INHERITANCES

SCRIPTURE: *"The boundary lines have fallen for me in pleasant places; surely I have a delightful inheritance." (Psalms 16:6 NIV)*

PRAYER: Father Your word declares that *"as His divine power has given to us all things that pertain to life and godliness, through the knowledge of Him who called us by glory and virtue,"* **(II Peter 1:3, NKJV).** Dear Lord thank You for my salvation, other pleasant gifts and the inheritances you have stored up for me. Please continue to bless me as You did for Jacob who said to Essau *"………God has been gracious to me and I have all I need."* **(Genesis 33:11 NIV)**

ACTION: Let us continue to pray for God to supply all our needs and give us the spirit of contentment **(Phil 4:19; 4:11)**

_____

_____

Today is June 16th, Day #168 in year 2024.
There are 198 days remaining in year 2024.

LOVING AND OBEYING GOD'S LAWS

SCRIPTURE: *"I have obeyed your laws, for I love them very much."* (Psalms 119:167 NLT)

PRAYER: Father, please give us the grace to continue to love You and obey all Your commandments so that we can enjoy all the blessings associated with such obedience according to Your word in ***Deuteronomy 28: 2-14.***

ACTION: On this Father's Day give thanks to God the Father of fathers and honor all fathers by praying for them to lead their family in serving God, loving Him and obeying His laws as admonished in God's word in *(Joshua 1:8)*. HAPPY FATHER'S DAY TO ALL.

_____

_____

Today is June 17th, Day #169 in year 2024.
There are 197 days remaining in year 2024.

SURROUNDED BY EMMANUEL

SCRIPTURE: *"I know the Lord is always with me. I will not be shaken, for he is right beside me." **(Psalms 16:8 NLT)***

PRAYER: Father, Your word declares. *"...You, O LORD, are a shield about me, my glory, and the lifter of my head. **(Psa. 3:3)***. Please Lord, surround me with Your shield that cannot be shaken or broken by the enemy.

ACTION: Let us prayerfully claim *Psalm 84:11* daily

Today is June 18th, Day #170 in year 2024.
There are 196 days remaining in year 2024.

CRYING TO CHRIST FOR DIVINE UNDERSTANDING

SCRIPTURE: *"Let my cry come near before thee, O Jehovah: Give me understanding according to thy word." (Psalms 119:169 ASV).*

PRAYER: Father, Your word declares. *"With God are wisdom and might; he has counsel and understanding" (Job 12:13).* Dear Lord, as You are liberal in giving wisdom *(James. 1:5)*; please, by Your divine power, increase my understanding of Your words, and Your ways in Jesus' name

ACTION: Let us claim Rom 8:32 and pray for God to give us all things we need to do greater exploits to glorify Him

Today is June 19th, Day #171 in year 2024.
There are 195 days remaining in year 2024.

PRAYER FOR DELIVERANCE AS PROMISED

SCRIPTURE: *"May my supplication come before you; deliver me according to your promise." **(Psalms 119:170 NIV)***

PRAYER: Father, Your word declares. *"Behold, I have given you authority to tread on serpents and scorpions, and over all the power of the enemy, and nothing shall hurt you" **(Luke 10:19)**.* Oh LORD, please deliver me from all troubles, afflictions and out of the hands of Satan and all enemies in Jesus' name.

ACTION: Thank God for His promise to answer our prayers *(Jer 33:3)*.

**Today is June 20th, Day #172 in year 2024.
There are 194 days remaining in year 2024.**

BEWEAR OF TEMPTATIONS

SCRIPTURE: *"AND [Jesus] said to His disciples, Temptations (snares, traps set to entice to sin) are sure to come, but woe to him by or through whom they come!"* **(Luke 17:1 AMPC)**.

PRAYER: Father, Your word declares. *"And lead us not into temptation but deliver us from evil: For thine is the kingdom, and the power, and the glory, forever. Amen."* **(Matt.6:13 KJV)**. Dear Lord, please don't let me tempt anyone or be tempted by anyone or anything. Empower me Oh God to overcome all temptations as Jesus Christ did **(Luke 4: 1-13)**

ACTION: Prayerfully resist the devil to put him to flight **(James 4:7)**

_____

_____

Today is June 21st, Day #173 in year 2024.
There are 193 days remaining in year 2024.

PROCLAIMING GOD'S RIGHTEOUS WORDS

SCRIPTURE: *"My tongue shall speak of Your word, For all Your commandments are righteousness." **(Psalm 119:172 NKJV)***

PRAYER: Father, thank You for Your word which are quick and powerful *(Heb 4:12)*; please give me the grace to meditate on Your word day and night, obey Your commandments and preach Your word in season and out of season *(2 Tim 4:2)* in Jesus' name

ACTION: Let us pray to profit from the word of God and be well equipped for every good work in line with ***2 Tim 3:16-17***

Today is June 22nd, Day #174 in year 2024.
There are 192 days remaining in year 2024.

CONVERSING WITH CHRIST

SCRIPTURE: *"Then Abram fell on his face, and God talked with him, saying:"* (**Gen. 17:3 NKJV**)

PRAYER: Father, what an honor and great privilege to be able to have conversation with You! As You did with Abram, please let me hear from You: *"... walk before Me and be blameless."* (**Gen. 17:1 NKJV**); *"...I will make My covenant between Me and you and will multiply you exceedingly." (Gen. 17:2 NKJV)*, etc. Dear Lord, please converse with me through Your word and any other way You want and give me the grace to be able to answer like Samuel who said: *".Speak, for Your servant hears." (I Samuel 3:10 NKJV)*.

ACTION: Pray for the grace to always hear from God

_____

_____

**Today is June 23rd, Day #175 in year 2024.
There are 191 days remaining in year 2024.**

ACCOMPLISHING GODLY ASSIGNMENTS

SCRIPTURE: *"I have glorified You on the earth. I have finished the work which You have given Me to do."* (John 17:4 NKJV).

PRAYER: Father, Your word declares, *"....Go into all the world and preach the gospel to every creature……" **(Mark 16:15 NKJV)*** and to *"...Go therefore and make disciples of all the nations, baptizing them in the name of the Father and of the Son and of the Holy Spirit, teaching them to observe all things that I have commanded you; and lo, I am with you always, even to the end of the age." Amen. **(Matthew 28:19-20 NKJV)***. Dear Lord, please empower me to satisfactorily accomplish all the assignments you have destined me to do in my lifetime.

ACTION: Pray for more diligence in doing God's work so as to finish like Jesus *(John 19:30)* and Apostle Paul *(2 Tim 4:7-8)*

**Today is June 24th, Day #176 in year 2024.
There are 190 days remaining in year 2024**

NEED A CHANGE OF NAME?

SCRIPTURE: *"No longer shall your name be called Abram, but your name shall be Abraham; for I have made you a father of many nations."* ***(Genesis 17:5 NKJV)***

PRAYER: Father, Your name change of 'Abram' to "Abraham" resulted in his status change from fruitlessness to fruitfulness akin to a change from 'negative' to 'positive' or 'scarcity' to 'surplus' etc.
Almighty God as You did for Abraham, please change my status from 'little faith' to 'giant faith'; from 'few won souls to 'multitude of won souls; from 'sickness' to 'excellent health'; from 'scanty good things' to 'abundant good things'; etc.

ACTION: Let us pray that God will change everything about us to glorify Him and positively enhance our lives.

_____

_____

Today is June 25th, Day #177 in year 2024.
There are 189 days remaining in year 2024.

DIVINE CARE AND PROVIDENCE

SCRIPTURE: *"And the ravens brought him bread and meat in the morning, and bread and meat in the evening, and he drank from the brook." (1 Kings 17:6)*

PRAYER: Father, as You divinely arranged for a raven bird to feed prophet Elijah *(1 kings 17:1-13)*; please Lord, by Your supernatural power, continue to supply all my needs according to Your riches in glory by Christ Jesus *(Phil 4:19)*

ACTION: Pray never to suffer famine nor lack any good thing *(Pro 10:3; Psa. 34:10)*

_____

_____

Today is June 26th, Day #178 in year 2024.
There are 188 days remaining in year 2024.

TRUSTING AND HOPING IN THE LORD

SCRIPTURE: *"Blessed is the person who trusts the Lord. The Lord will be his confidence." **(Jeremiah 17:7 GW)***

PRAYER: Father, Your word declares: *"Those who trust in the Lord are as Mount Zion, which cannot be moved but abides forever."* ***(Psa 125:1)***. Please give me the grace to trust You and put my hope in You so that You can be my confidence in Jesus name

ACTION: Let us determine to trust the Lord wholeheartedly

Today is June 27th, Day #179 in year 2024.
There are 187 days remaining in year 2024.

KEPT UNDER GOD'S EYES AND WINGS

SCRIPTURE: *"Keep me as the apple of Your eye; Hide me under the shadow of Your wings," **(Psalms 17:8 NKJV).***

PRAYER: Father, Your word declares, *"He who dwells in the secret place of the Most High Shall abide under the shadow of the Almighty." **(Psa. 91:1 NKJV)**.* Oh Lord, please keep me protected and safe under Your watchful eyes such that whoever touches me will touch the apple of Your eye ***(Zechariah 2:8, NKJV)***.

ACTION: Let us thank God and pray that we'll never do anything that will make God take His eyes away from us

**Today is June 28th, Day #180 in year 2024.
There are 186 days remaining in year 2024**

REWARDS FOR RIGHTEOUSNESS AND DOING GOOD

SCRIPTURE: *"Righteous people continue to do things that are right. People who do good things become stronger." **(Job 17:9 EASY)***

PRAYER: Father, Your word declares, *"Whoever pursues righteousness and love finds life, prosperity and honor."* ***(Pro. 21:21 NIV)*** and that we should not be weary in doing good, for at the proper time we will reap a harvest if we do not give up ***(Gal. 6:9 NIV)***. Almighty God, please empower me to pursue righteousness and to do good always in Jesus name.

ACTION: Pray light of God in you manifest righteousness and goodness in all that you do ***(Eph 6:9)***

_____

_____

**Today is June 29th, Day #181 in year 2024.
There are 185 days remaining in year 2024.**

SOLOMON'S DAILY FOOD SUPPLIED

SCRIPTURE: *"Solomon's food supply for one day was 180 bushels of flour, 360 bushels of coarse flour, 10 fattened cows, 20 cows from the pasture, and 100 sheep in addition to deer, gazelles, fallow deer, and fattened birds." (1 Kings 4:22-23 GW)*

PRAYER: Father, Your word declares, *"Give us this day our daily bread." (Matthew 6:11)*.
Oh Lord, as You did for Solomon, please bless me abundantly and empower me to feed my household adequately well and as many needy people as possible in Jesus' name.

ACTION: Prayerfully learn about the secret to Solomon's success as a king in *1 Kings 3: 3-15* and consider emulating Solomon.

_____

_____

**Today is June 30th, Day #182 in year 2024.
There are 184 days remaining in year 2024**

FAITHFUL FRIENDSHIP

SCRIPTURE: *"Now when he had finished speaking to Saul, the soul of Jonathan was knit to the soul of David, and Jonathan loved him as his own soul." (I Samuel 18:1 NKJV).*

PRAYER: Father, Your word declares, *"A man who has friends must himself be friendly, But there is a friend who sticks closer than a brother." (Proverbs 18:24 NKJV).* Oh Lord, I thank You for Your Son Jesus Christ my greatest Friend who loved me and laid down His life for me *(John 15:13-15).* Please let all our human-to-human friendships be Godly and manifest mutual strong faith, loyalty, honesty, kindness, hospitality, etc. akin to friendship between Jonathan and David *(1 Sam 18:1-3; 1 Sam 20:1-42)*

ACTION: Let us pray to be a friend that loves at all times *(Pro 17:17).*

_____

_____

JULY

Today is July 1st, Day #183 in year 2024.
There are 183 days remaining in year 2024

NAMING BABIES WITH GOOD NAMES

SCRIPTURE: *"When Lamech was 182 years old, he became the father of a son. He named him Noah [Relief], and said, "This child will bring us relief from the work and painful labor of our hands since the Lord has cursed the ground." (Gen. 5:28-29 GW).*

PRAYER: Please help us to give appropriate Godly names to our babies as did the 'righteous' Lamech in the Bible who was son of Methuselah and father of Noah. The name 'Noah' Lamech gave his son is similar in sound to the Hebrew word for 'Comfort' *(See Gen. 25:29)*.

ACTION: Prayerfully choose names that will glorify God for your babies who are 'heritage of God' *(Psa. 127:3)*

_____

_____

Today is July 2nd, Day #184 in year 2024.
There are 182 days remaining in year 2024

PERSISTING IN PRAYER

SCRIPTURE: *"And there was a widow in that city; and she came unto him, saying, Avenge me of mine adversary"* ***(Luke 18:3)***

PRAYER: Father, Your word declares that we should pray without ceasing ***(1 Thes 5:17)***; Oh Lord, please empower me to redouble, reinforce and be more persistent in my prayer life so as to provoke rapid answers as happened for the widow in the parable of the persistent widow ***(Luke 18:1-8)***

ACTION: Let us strive to pray more ***(Rom 15:30)***

Today is July 3rd, Day #185 in year 2024.
There are 181 days remaining in year 2024

GIVEN TO HOSPITALITY

SCRIPTURE: *"Please let a little water be brought, and wash your feet, and rest yourselves under the tree." **(Gen 18:4 NKJV)***

PRAYER: Father, Your word declares *"Do not forget to show hospitality to strangers, for by so doing some people have shown hospitality to angels without knowing it." **(Hebrews. 13:2 NIV).***
Dear Lord, please give me the grace, the resources and the designing spirit to be hospitable and blessed like Abraham in Jesus name

ACTION: Let us practice hospitality *(Rom 23:13)*

_____
_____

**Today is July 4th, Day #186 in year 2024.
There are 180 /days remaining in year 2024**

SHAMEFUL DEFEAT OF SENNACHERIB

SCRIPTURE: *"That night the angel of the Lord went out to the Assyrian camp and killed 185,000 Assyrian soldiers. When the surviving Assyrians woke up the next morning, they found corpses everywhere." **(2 Kings 19:35 NLT)***

PRAYER: Father, Sennacherib, king of Assyria, defied You and Israel and, the night before he could attack Israel, You sent an Angel that killed 185,000 of Assyrian soldiers. Thereafter, Sennacherib himself was killed with sword by his two sons as he was worshipping in the house of Nisroch, his god. *(2 Kings 19:8-37)*. Oh Lord, please fight for me against all 'Sennacherib and Assyrian' enemies of my life in Jesus name.

ACTION: Let's claim the scripture *Jer 1:19* that no one will prevail against you

_____

_____

Today is July 5th, Day #187 in year 2024.
There are 179 days remaining in year 2024.

CAUSING NO CHILD TO STUMBLE FROM CHRIST

SCRIPTURE: *"but whoever causes one of these little ones who believe in Me to stumble and sin [by leading him away from My teaching], it would be better for him to have a heavy millstone [as large as one turned by a donkey] hung around his neck and to be drowned in the depth of the sea." (Matt. 18:6 AMP)*.

PRAYER: Father Your word declares *"Behold, children are a heritage and gift from the Lord……." (Psa. 127:3 AMP)*, and, *"Allow the children to come to Me, and do not forbid them, for the kingdom of God belongs to such as these." (Luke 18:16)*, Please Lord, give me the strategy, wisdom and wherewithal with which to draw children and young people to You and never to scare them away or forbid them from coming to you in Jesus name.

ACTION: Let charity begin from home by ensuring our biological children give their lives to Jesus Christ and are taught to serve Him as did Abraham concerning his children *(Gen 18:19)*.

_____

_____

Today is July 6th, Day #188 in year 2024.
There are 178 days remaining in year 2024.

JUNK THAT JEALOUSY

SCRIPTURE: *"And the women answered one another as they played, and said, Saul hath slain his thousands, And David his ten thousands. And Saul was very wroth, and the saying displeased him; and he said, They have ascribed unto David ten thousands, and to me they have ascribed but thousands: and what can he have more but the kingdom? And Saul eyed David from that day and forward. And it came to pass on the morrow, that the evil spirit from God came upon Saul, and he prophesied in the midst of the house: and David played with his hand, as at other times: and there was a javelin in Saul's hand. And Saul cast the javelin; for he said, I will smite David even to the wall with it. And David avoided out of his presence twice. And Saul was afraid of David, because the LORD was with him, and was departed from Saul."* **(1 Samuel 18:7-12 KJV)**

PRAYER: Father Your word declares *"For jealousy makes a man furious, and he will not spare when he takes revenge"* ***(Pro 6:34)***, and that bitter jealousy and selfish ambition is unspiritual, demonic and full of vile practices ***(see James 3:14-16)***. Please Lord, deliver us from bitter jealousy of which Saul became a victim and was determined to kill David ***(1 Sam 19)***.

ACTION: Prayerfully junk every trace of jealousy in you today

**Today is July 7th, Day #189 in year 2024.
There are 177 days remaining in year 2024**

GIVE UP GOSSIPING

SCRIPTURE: *"The words of a whisperer or talebearer are as dainty morsels; they go down into the innermost parts of the body." **(Proverbs 18:8 AMPC)***

PRAYER: Father Your word declares *"Death and life are in the power of the tongue, and those who love it will eat its fruits"* ***(Pro. 18:21)*** and that *"Whoso privily slandereth his neighbour, Him will I cut off....,"* ***(Psalm 101:5 KJV).*** Almighty God, please don't let me be an object or subject of gossiping Jesus name.

ACTION: Let us prayerfully obey the injunction in ***(Ephesians 4:29 KJV)***

_____

_____

**Today is July 8th, Day #190 in year 2024.
There are 176 days remaining in year 2024.**

AVOIDING ABOMINATIONS

SCRIPTURE: *"When thou art come into the land which the LORD thy God giveth thee, thou shalt not learn to do after the abominations of those nations." **(Deuteronomy 18:9 KJV)**.*

PRAYER: Father, all sins that miss Your mark of perfection and can separate us from You are detestable to You and can be considered abominations. Examples of abominable things to You include wickedness, adultery, idolatry, unfair scales, haughty eyes, false witnessing, innocent shedding of blood, etc. Oh Lord, please don't let me be associated with anything abominable to You. By Your power let all evil abominations be eradicated in our communities in Jesus name

ACTION: Prayerfully check out and avoid the 7 things listed as abomination to God *(Pro 6: 16-19)*.

_____

_____

**Today is July 9th, Day #191 in year 2024.
There are 175 days remaining in year 2024**

POWERLESS 'PILATE'

SCRIPTURE: *"Then Pilate said to Him, "Are You not speaking to me? Do You not know that I have power to crucify You, and power to release You?" Jesus answered, "You could have no power at all against Me unless it had been given you from above. Therefore, the one who delivered Me to you has the greater sin." (John 19:10-11 NKJV).*

PRAYER: Father thank You because You are Omnipotent, meaning You are infinite in power, has unlimited authority and all power belongs to You *(Rev 19:6, Psa 62:11)*. Dear Lord, let anyone trying to use his/her position and/or power to harm or kill us fail woefully and, as You did to Pilate, let such people know that without Your permission their mission cannot succeed in Jesus' name.

ACTION: Fear no one, just pray and claim *1 John 4:4* and Command all 'Pilate' in Your life to park and go now.

_____

_____

Today is July 10th, Day #192 in year 2024.
There are 174 days remaining in year 2024

ABIDING UNDER THE SHADOW OF THE ALMIGHTY

SCRIPTURE: *"He who dwells in the secret place of the Most High, Shall abide under the shadow of the Almighty." (Psa. 91:1 NKJV)*

PRAYER: Oh Most High and The Almighty God, thank You for being my Maker, my Savior, my Shield and my Buckler; please let me continue to dwell and abide in You faithfully so that all Your blessings described in *Psalm 91:3-16* shall be mine in Jesus name

ACTION: Let us thank God that we belong to Him.

Today is July 11th, Day #193 in year 2024.
There are 173 days remaining in year 2024

DON'T SUCCUMB TO MARRIAGE DIVORCE

SCRIPTURE: *The Pharisees also came to Him, testing Him, and saying to Him, "Is it lawful for a man to divorce his wife for just any reason?"* ***(Matt. 19:3, NKJV)***

PRAYER: Father when you put the institution of marriage in place it was not meant for divorce as evident in Your word that says *"You hate divorce"* ***(Mal. 2:16)*** and that, *"......Therefore, what God has joined together, let not man separate." **(Matt 19: 4-6)***. Omnipotent God, please curtail the attack of Satan on all marriages that is responsible for today's avalanche of divorces in our society. Please let married couples hate what you hate such that instead of rushing to divorce each other they will prayerfully consider reconciliation and do your will to uphold their marriage vow and stay married

ACTION: Prayerfully determine not to be the one that will put asunder what God has joined together.

_____

_____

Today is July 12th, Day #194 in year 2024.
There are 172 days remaining in year 2024

GOING 'UP' TO GOD

SCRIPTURE: *"And Moses went up unto God, and the LORD called unto him out of the mountain, saying, Thus shalt thou say to the house of Jacob, and tell the children of Israel"* **(Exodus 19:3)**

PRAYER: Father, thank You for making Yourself available to us as Your people. When Moses came up to You in the wilderness of Sinai You sent him to tell the Israelites that *"... if ye will obey my voice indeed, and keep my covenant, then ye shall be a peculiar treasure unto me above all people: for all the earth is mine:"* **(Exo 19:5)**.
Please Lord, give us the grace to come 'up' to You by praying, praising and serving You more fervently and more diligently in Jesus name.

ACTION: Let us strife to go 'up' to God every day. Peculiar people must prayerfully do good and peculiar things.

_____
_____

Today is July 13th, Day #195 in year 2024. There are 171 days remaining in year 2024

DIVORCE IS NOT A DIVINE AGENDA

SCRIPTURE: *"Some Pharisees came and tried to trap him with this question: "Should a man be allowed to divorce his wife for just any reason?" **(Matt. 19:3 NLT)***

PRAYER: Father, Your divine arrangement for marriage is for cleaving together and not for separation or divorce for Your word declares *".... a man shall leave his father and mother and be joined to his wife, and the two shall become one flesh' So then, they are no longer two but one flesh. Therefore, what God has joined together, let not man separate." **(Matthew 19:5-6 NKJV)***. Furthermore, the Bible declares that *"... the Lord God of Israel says That He hates divorce,......" **(Mal.2:16 NKJV)***. Oh Lord, please don't let adultery or any other factor open the door for divorce or separation to creep into our marriages as this will mean violation of Your ordinance

ACTION: Let us pray that the mercy of God will bring about reconciliation and restoration for all marriages that have faced or are facing divorce

_____

_____

Today is July 14th, Day #196 in year 2024.
There are 170 days remaining in year 2024

BURNING CHILDREN TO BAAL

SCRIPTURE: *"They have built also the high places of Baal, to burn their sons with fire for burnt offerings unto Baal, which I commanded not, nor speak, neither came it into my mind: (Jeremiah 19:5, KJV)*

PRAYER: Father, ritual child sacrifices and sale of body parts is, sadly to say, alive and growing in many countries of the world. Dear Lord, since children are Your heritage *(Psa 127:3)* and Your commandment is against burning or killing children for rituals *(Jer. 19)*, please, by Your great power, defend, save and deliver all children from been killed by blood sucking ritualists in Jesus' name

ACTION: Let us pray against evil activities of ritualists and report suspected activities to appropriate authority

Today is July 15th, Day #197 in year 2024.
There are 169 days remaining in year 2024

ANOINTED HANDS

SCRIPTURE: *"And when Paul had laid hands on them, the Holy Spirit came upon them, and they spoke with tongues and prophesied." **(Acts 19:6 NKJV)***

PRAYER: Father, according to Your word, many signs shall follow those who believe in You including *"they shall lay hands on the sick, and they shall recover." **(Mark 16:18b)***. Oh Lord please anoint me afresh and let my hands be a conductor of Your miracles akin to that of Jesus ***(Luke 13:11-13)***; and of Paul's ***(Acts 8:17; 19:6)***

ACTION: Lift up your palms and pray God to anoint you afresh to do greater exploits.

_____

_____

Today is July 16th, Day #198 in year 2024.
There are 168 days remaining in year 2024

POWER AND PERFECTION OF GOD'S LAW AND TESTIMONY

SCRIPTURE: *"The law of the Lord is perfect, converting the soul; The testimony of the Lord is sure, making wise the simple;" **(Psa. 19:7 NKJV)***

PRAYER: Father, Your word declares: ...*"All Scripture is given by inspiration of God, and is profitable for doctrine, for reproof, for correction, for instruction in righteousness, that the man of God may be complete, thoroughly equipped for every good work." **(II Tim. 3:16-17 NKJV)***. Oh Lord, please let the power, perfection and all the divine attributes of Your word (laws, statutes, commandments, etc) convert our souls and make us wise to live holy, serve You diligently and do Your will at all times in Jesus name

ACTION: Let's obey the mandate in ***Joshua 1:8***

_____

_____

Today is July 17th, Day #199 in year 2024.
There are 167 days remaining in year 2024

SEEKING SALVATION DESPERATELY AND SINCERELY

SCRIPTURE: *"And Jesus said to him, "Today salvation has come to this house, because he also is a son of Abraham;"* **(Luke 19:9)**

PRAYER: Father, Your word declares, *"But from there you will seek the LORD your God, and you will find Him if you seek Him with all your heart and with all your soul." (Deut. 4:29, NIV).* Thank You Lord Jesus for coming in to this world to *"..seek and to save that which was lost"* **(Luke 19:10b).** An example of Your good gesture is Zacchaeus the rich chief Publican who sought You desperately by climbing up into a sycamore tree (due to his short stature) to see You. Seeing Zacchaeus' efforts and desire to have an encounter with You, said to him *" Zacchaeus, make haste and come down; for today I must abide at thy house"* **(Luke 19: 5).** Zacchaeus received Jesus joyfully to his house and was repentant. and promised to restitute for anything he has taken wrongly. The end result is that Zacchaeus sought Jesus Christ desperately and sincerely and received salvation for himself and possibly his entire household. Dear Lord, let multitude of unsaved souls seek Jesus Christ sincerely and desperately like Zacchaeus in order to receive salvation in Jesus name

ACTION: As one who has been redeemed, you are saved to serve in terms of helping the unsaved, get saved *(Roman 10:14)*. Prayerfully determine to carry out this assignment.

_____

_____

Today is July 18th, Day #200 in year 2024.
There are 166 days remaining in year 2024

LOSING HOPE AND CONFIDENCE IN THE LORD?

SCRIPTURE: *"He hath stripped me of my glory, and taken the crown from my head." **(Job 19:9)***

PRAYER: Father, Your word declares that You will never live me nor forsake me ***(Heb 13:5)*** Please Lord, don't let life's circumstances and what people say discourage me and provoke me to make wrong judgment and unfounded accusation about You and Your role in my life in Jesus name

ACTION: As believers in the Lord Let us thank God and claim His promise about us in ***Isa 43:1-4***

_____

_____

Today is July 19th, Day #201 in year 2024.
There are 165 days remaining in year 2024

TRANSFER OF THE ARK OF GOD TO THE NEW TABERNACLE

SCRIPTURE: *"David assembled all Israel in Jerusalem to bring up the ark of the Lord to the place he had prepared for it. He called together the descendants of Aaron and the Levites: from the descendants of Elizaphan, Shemaiah the leader and 200 relatives;"* ***(1 Chron 15:3-4, 8 NIV)***

PRAYER: Father, among the 800 plus people (Levites) David recruited to transfer the Ark of God to a new Tabernacle was Shemaiah, who was the leader of 200 members of the Subclan of Elizaphan ***(1 Chron 15:3-11, TLB)***. Dear Lord, please let my family and our descendants always be privileged to serve You with gladness including partaking in 'building Your Church' ***(Mt 16:18)***

ACTION: Aspire to be among the few chosen when many are called to do God's work.

_____

_____

Today is July 20th, Day #202 in year 2024.
There are 164 days remaining in year 2024

PRAYING FROM THE PSALMS

SCRIPTURE: *"May the Lord answer you when you are in distress; may the name of the God of Jacob protect you." (Psalms 20:1 NIV)*

PRAYER: Father, thank You for Your word (the Bible) that You enjoined us not to let depart from our mouth, but *"..to meditate in it day and night, that you may observe to do according to all that is written in it. For then you will make your way prosperous, and then you will have good success." (Joshua 1:8 NKJV)*. Please Lord, help us to emulate David in praying to You and praising You as he did and has documented in several chapters of the book of Psalms including the following prayer points in **Psalm 20: 1-5**:
"May the Lord answer you in the day of trouble;
May the name of the God of Jacob defend you;
May He send you help from the sanctuary,
And strengthen you out of Zion;
May He remember all your offerings,
May He grant you according to your heart's desire, And fulfill all your purpose. And in the name of our God we will set up our banners!
May the Lord fulfill all your petitions."*(Psalms 20:1-5 NKJV)*

ACTION: Prayerfully ask Jesus to teach you how to pray. *(Luke 11:1)*

Today is July 21st, Day #203 in year 2024.
There are 163 days remaining in year 2024

PREACHING THE GOSPEL EVERY PLACE

SCRIPTURE: *"He visited many places in that region. He spoke to the believers in each place. He helped them to be strong. After that, he arrived in Greece." **(Acts 20:2 EASY)***

PRAYER: Father, Your word declares, *".....Go ye into all the world, and preach the gospel to every creature." **(Mark 16:15)***
Oh Lord God, please help us to be more diligent and assiduous, in spreading the gospel and encouraging the believers in many places as Paul and other early believers did *(Acts chap 20)*

ACTION: Let us do as Apostle Paul suggests in *2 Tim 2:42*

**Today is July 22nd, Day #204 in year 2024.
There are 162 days remaining in year 2024**

STOP THE STRIFE

SCRIPTURE: *"It is honorable for a man to stop striving, since any fool can start a quarrel."* **Proverbs 20:3 NKJV**

PRAYER: Father, Your word declares, *"..,avoid foolish and ignorant disputes, knowing that they generate strife."* ***(II Timothy 2:23 NKJV)*** and *"He who is of a proud heart stirs up strife, But he who trusts in the Lord will be prospered." **(Prov.28:25 NKJV)***. Dear Lord, please prevent and/or stop strife in all our relationships for strife is a sign of worldliness and carnality as Apostle Paul indicates in ***1 Cor 3:3***

ACTION: Let us prayerfully pursue love instead of strife

_____

_____

Today is July 23rd, Day #205 in year 2024.
There are 161 days remaining in year 2024

GATHERING TOGETHER TO SEEK HELP FROM GOD

SCRIPTURE: *"So Judah gathered together to ask help from the Lord; and from all the cities of Judah they came to seek the Lord."* **(II CHRON 20:4)**

PRAYER: Father, Your word declares, *"not forsaking the assembling of ourselves together, as is the manner of some, but exhorting one another, ..."* **(Heb. 10:25 NKJV)**, and that *"One man can chase away 1,000 of my people! Two men can chase away 10,000 of them! ...."* **(Deut. 32:30 EASY)**. Dear Lord, please help us to seek Your help together as a team so that we can do greater exploits and be able to defeat our enemies as You helped Judah and Jerusalem to do **(II Chron. Chap 20)**

ACTION: Let us prayerfully do our part to promote unity.

Today is July 24th, Day #206 in year 2024.
There are 160 days remaining in year 2024.

REJOICING IN GOD'S SALVATION AND VICTORY

SCRIPTURE: *"We will rejoice in your salvation, And in the name of our God we will set up our banners! May the Lord fulfill all your petitions."* ***(Psalms 20:5 NKJV)***

PRAYER: Father, Your word declares *"Glad songs of salvation are in the tents of the righteous: "The right hand of the Lord does valiantly **(Psa 118:15)**.* Dear Lord, please let us always remember to give thanks to You for all things especially for our salvation, victory over our enemies and Your answers to our petitions in Jesus' name

ACTION: Let us do what ***Eph 5:20***, says: *"Giving thanks always...."*

_____
_____

Today is July 25th, Day #207 in year 2024.
There are 159 days remaining in year 2024

GOD SAVES AND ANSWERS HIS ANOINTED

SCRIPTURE: *"Now I know that the Lord saves His anointed; He will answer him from His holy heaven With the saving strength of His right hand."* ***(Psalms 20:6 NKJV).***

PRAYER: Father, thank You for Jesus Christ who is the ultimate Anointed One ***(Acts 10:38)***, LORD, by Your grace we also have become God's anointed by believing and receiving Jesus Christ as our Lord and Savior, thereby becoming Joint heirs with Him ***(Rom 8:17)***. Therefore,
as Your anointed one, Lord please keep me save from all evils at all times and answer me from Your Holy heaven in Jesus name.

ACTION: To become God's anointed, you must believe in Jesus Christ and give your life to Him today

_____

_____

Today is July 26th, Day #208 in year 2024.
There are 158 days remaining in year 2024

BLESSED ARE CHILDREN OF A RIGHTEOUS MAN WITH INTEGRITY

SCRIPTURE: *"A righteous man that walketh in his integrity, Blessed are his children after him." **(Proverbs 20:7 ASV)***

PRAYER: Father, please empower me to live a life of righteousness with high integrity that will glorify You and prepare the way for my descendants to be blessed from generation to generation in Jesus name

ACTION: Thank Jesus Christ for making your righteousness possible

_____

_____

Today is July 27th, Day #209 in year 2024.
There are 157 days remaining in year 2024.

COMPLETE AND CAREFULLY OBEYING GOD'S COMMANDS?

SCRIPTURE: *"Take the rod; you and your brother Aaron gather the congregation together. Speak to the rock before their eyes, and it will yield its water; thus you shall bring water for them out of the rock, and give drink to the congregation and their animals." (Num20:8 NKJV)*

PRAYER: Father, whatever You command us to do, please give us the grace to carefully and completely do as Your require. Please Lord, don't let anger or any other factor rob us of fulfilling our destiny and reaching the 'promised land' as it did to Moses who was denied entry into the promised land because, out of anger, he smote the rock instead of speaking to it as You commanded him to do to provide water for the Israelites and their animals in the wilderness *(Num 20: 9-13)*

ACTION: Don't 'Smite at' what you are supposed to 'Speak to'. Do your best to obey God and his servants 100 percent and nothing less

_____

_____

**Today is July 28th, Day #210 in the year 2024.
There are 156 days remaining in year 2024**

HONORING PARENTS

SCRIPTURE: *"For everyone who curses his father, or his mother shall surely be put to death. He has cursed his father or his mother. His blood shall be upon him." **(Leviticus 20:9 NKJV)***

PRAYER: Father, please let our children obey Your commandment to not curse their parents. Instead of cursing their parents, let our children honor their parents so that their days may be long upon the land which the LORD their God has giveth them ***(Exodus 20:12)***.

ACTION: Let love, unity and praying for one another be prominent in your family.

_____

_____

Today is July 29th, Day #211 in year 2024.
There are 155 days remaining in year 2024

EXILES RETURNING TO JERUSALEM WITH EZRA

SCRIPTURE: *"These are the leaders of the families and the genealogy of those who left Babylon with me (Ezra) during the reign of King Artaxerxes: from the family of Joab: Obadiah, son of Jehiel, with 210 males"* ***(Ezra 8:1, 9 GW)***

PRAYER: Father, out of the 1434 exiles who returned to Jerusalem from Babylonian captivity under Prophet Ezra's supervision, 210 of them were of Joab's family, their leader been Obadiah the son of Jehiel ***(Ezra 8:9-10)***. Almighty God, please don't let me or any member of my family be in any form of 'Babylonian captivity', physical or spiritual

ACTION: Let's give thanks to God for His grace that has liberated us from the captivity of sins.

Today is July 30th, Day #212 in year 2024.
There are 154 days remaining in year 2024

GOD'S WAY TO STAY SAFE AND PROTECTED

SCRIPTURE: *"You will know the right thing to do, and that will keep you safe." **(Pro. 2:11 EASY)***

PRAYER: Father, Your word declares: *"Do not forsake wisdom, and she will protect you; love her, and she will watch over you." **(Pro 2:11 NIV)***. Dear Lord please give me foresight, wisdom, understanding and all that I need to stay safe, and preserved in Your everlasting arms

ACTION: Let's is prayerfully seek to live, move and have our being in the LORD *(Acts 17:28a)*

_____
_____

Today is July 31st, Day #213 in year 2024.
There are 153 days remaining in year 2024

GOD IS A GENEROUS GIVER

SCRIPTURE: *"You have given him his heart's desire, And have not withheld the request of his lips. Selah"* **(Psalms 21:2 NKJV)**

PRAYER: Father, Your word declares: *"Every good gift and every perfect gift is from above, and cometh down from the Father of lights, with whom is no variableness, neither shadow of turning." **(James 1:17 KJV)***. Dear Lord, as You did to the king in **Psalm 21** (David?), please give me my heart's desires and withhold not the request of my lips in Jesus' name.

ACTION: Let's thank God for seeing the last day of July and all He did for us in the 7th month. Pray for smooth and safe transitioning to August

_____

_____

AUGUST

**Today is August 1st, Day #214 in year 2024.
There are 152 days remaining in year 2024**

GOD'S BLESSINGS OF HONOR AND GOODNESS

SCRIPTURE: *"For You meet him with the blessings of goodness; You set a crown of pure go ld upon his head." (Psa. 21:3 NKJV)*

PRAYER: Father, thank You for word declare that You have made us kings and priests unto Yourself *(Rev. 1:6)*. Dear Lord, as You did for that king in *Psalm 21:3*, please endow me with the blessings of goodness and crown my head with honor and glory *(Psalms 21:3 NKJV)*

ACTION: Let us give thanks to God who has preserved our lives to see the new month of August

_____

_____

**Today is August 2nd, Day #215 in year 2024.
There are 151 days remaining in year 2024.**

GIVING GOD THE BEST GIFTS

SCRIPTURE: *"For they have given a tiny part of their surplus, but she, poor as she is, has given everything she has." **(Luke 21:4 NLT)***

PRAYER: Father, thank You for giving us Your best (Your Son, Jesus Christ) to save our souls ***(John 3:16)***. Oh Lord, please help us to learn from Your example and do our best to give You the best gifts (offerings, tithes, services, etc.) as did the poor widow in today's lead Scripture above

ACTION: What we give determines what we get ***(Luke 6:38)***. Let us prayerfully determine to give God our best gifts,

_____

_____

**Today is August 3rd, Day #216 in the year 2024.
There are 150 days remaining in year 2024**

FREEING THE WORLD FROM FLOODWATERS

SCRIPTURE: *"And the floodwaters covered the earth for 150 days." **(Genesis 7:24 NLT)***

PRAYER: Father, thank You for Your mercy and Your promise not to destroy the world again by floodwaters beyond the one You stopped after 150 days of flooding and destruction of human beings **(Gen 7:1-24)**. Father, On the day of the LORD'S wrath; when *"..all the earth will be devoured in the fire of His jealousy,..."* **(Zeph 1:18)**, please don't let me be among those that will be consumed in the fire in Jesus name

ACTION: Let us pray against global warming turning to world destruction by fire

_____

_____

Today is August 4th, Day #217 in the year 2024. There are 149 days remaining in year 2024

DO LIKE GOD: HATE DIVORCE

SCRIPTURE: *"For the Lord God of Israel says That He hates divorce, For it covers one's garment with violence,"* Says the Lord of hosts. *"Therefore, take heed to your spirit, That you do not deal treacherously." **(Malachi 2:16 NKJV)***

PRAYER: Father, Your word declares *"So then, they are no longer two but one flesh. Therefore, what God has joined together, let not man separate." **(Matthew 19:6 NKJV)***. Oh Lord, in our marriages, please have mercy and help us to pursue reconciliation instead of divorce so as not to do what You hate

ACTION: Satan is a Separator; pray him out of your marriage ***(James 4:7)***

_____

_____

Today is August 5th, Day #218 in year 2024. There are 148 days remaining in year 2024

HOW JESUS WAS ABLE TO BRING FORGIVENESS FOR PEOPLE'S SINS

SCRIPTURE: *"For this reason, Jesus had to be made like us, his brothers and sisters, in every way. He became like people so that he could be their merciful and faithful high priest in service to God. Then he could bring forgiveness for the people's sins." (Hebrews 2:17 ERV)*

PRAYER: Father, Your word declares *"Christ had no sin, but God made him become sin so that in Christ we could be right with God." (2 Cor. 5:21 ERV)*. Oh Lord, thank You for Your sacrifice and work of redemption that made it possible for our sins to be forgivable if we confess and repent of them. Please give us the grace to live holy like You in Jesus name *(1 Peter 1:16)*

ACTION: Give thanks to Jesus Christ daily for your redemption *(Rom. 3: 24)*

**Today is August 6th, Day #219 in year 2024.
There are 147 days remaining in year 2024**

CANDIDATES FOR THE SECOND DEATH?

SCRIPTURE: *"But the cowardly, unbelieving, abominable, murderers, sexually immoral, sorcerers, idolaters, and all liars shall have their part in the lake which burns with fire and brimstone, which is the second death."* ***(Revelation 21:8 NKJV)***

PRAYER: Father, the second death is also called the lake of fire which will be the final residence of the following eight categories of people: the cowardly, unbelieving, abominable, murderers, sexually immoral, sorcerers, idolaters, and all liars ***(Rev 20:14; 21:8)***.
Oh Lord, let our names be only in the Book of life and never among those to be in the lake of fire or second death

ACTION: To avoid the second death (having residence in the lake of fire) give your life to Jesus Christ, today or as soon as possible

_____
_____

Today is August 7th, Day #220 in year 2024.
There are 146 days remaining in year 2024

DANGER OF FORSAKING GOD

SCRIPTURE: *"Your own wickedness will correct you, And your backslidings will rebuke you. Know therefore and see that it is an evil and bitter thing That you have forsaken the Lord your God, And the fear of Me is not in you," Says the Lord God of hosts." **(Jeremiah 2:19 NKJV)**.*

PRAYER: Father, thank You for Your promise not to forsake me **(Heb 13:5)**; please don't let me ever forsake You so that it won't be my wickedness that will correct me, neither will it be my backsliding that will rebuke me in Jesus name.

ACTION: Let us determine to draw near to God that He May draw near to us **(James 4:8)**

_____

_____

Today is August 8th, Day #221 in year 2024.
There are 145 days remaining in year 2024.

SERVING AS "TEMPLE SERVANTS"

SCRIPTURE: *"and 220 temple servants. They were descended from the temple servants whom David and his officials had appointed to work for the Levites. These were all listed by name. (Ezra 8:20 GW)*

PRAYER: Father thank You for those who dedicate themselves to doing the works in your house. Examples include the 220 'temple servants' who were among the exiles that the Priest Ezra led to return from Babylon to Jerusalem to rebuild the temple *(Ezra Chap8)*. Oh Lord, please bless all church workers and take sicknesses away from them as Your word indicates in *Exodus 23:25-26*

ACTION: Prayerfully consider if there is something you can do to also be a 'servant of the temple' and partake in the blessings that appertain

_____

_____

**Today is August 9th, Day #222 in year 2024.
There are 144 days remaining in year 2024.**

THE LORD HAS DONE GREAT THINGS

SCRIPTURE: *"Don't be afraid, O land. Be glad now and rejoice, for the Lord has done great things."* **(Joel 2:21 NLT)**

PRAYER: Father, thank You for the great things You have done for me so far. As Your word declares *"Call to Me, and I will answer you, and show you great and mighty things, which you do not know.'"* **(Jer' 33:3 NKJV).** Dear Lord please continue to do and manifest greater things in all areas of our lives that will glorify You and give us joy unlimited in Jesus name

ACTION: Let us praise God greatly for He is a Great God who continues to do great things

Today is August 10th, Day #223 in year 2024.
There are 143 days remaining in year 2024

TEACHING AND SPREADING THE GOSPEL AS A TEAM

SCRIPTURE: *"But you know what kind of person Timothy proved to be. Like a father and son we worked hard together to spread the Good News." **(Phil 2:22 GW)***

PRAYER: Father, please help me to be an active team member in working hard together with other believers to spread the Good News of the Gospel as did Timothy in working together with Apostle Paul ***(Phil 2:19-22)***

ACTION: In terms of spreading the Good News of the Gospel let us prayerfully seek collaborations instead of divisions

_____

_____

**Today is August 11th, Day #224 in year 2024.
There are 142 days remaining in year 2024**

AVOIDING FOOLISH ARGUMENTS

SCRIPTURE: *"Don't have anything to do with foolish and stupid arguments. You know they cause quarrels." (2Tim. 2:23 GW)*

PRAYER: Father, please help us control our tongues and deliver us from needless, unholy and foolish arguments for Your word says *"..avoid foolish controversies, genealogies, dissensions, and quarrels about the law, for they are unprofitable and worthless"; "for it will lead people into more and more ungodliness,"* ***(Titus 3:9; 2 Tim 2:16)***. Oh LORD, my strength, and my redeemer, Let the words of my mouth, and the meditation of my heart, be acceptable in Your sight, in Jesus name. Amen ***(Psalms 19:14)***

ACTION: Let us prayerfully think before we talk to avoid conversations that can engender sins

_____

_____

Today is August 12th, Day #225 in year 2024.
There are 141 1days remaining in year 2024

'DOS' AND 'DONTS' OF GOD'S SERVANT

SCRIPTURE: *"And a servant of the Lord must not quarrel but be gentle to all, able to teach, patient,"* **(II Tim.2:24 NKJV)**

PRAYER: Father, Your word declares that *"with God all things are possible"* **(Luke 1:37)**. As one of Your servants, please help me to meet all the criteria required for serving You satisfactorily including those Apostle Paul laid down for Timothy his Prodigy: Servant of the Lord:
(a) must not strive
(b) be gentle unto all men,
(c) apt to teach, (d) patient,

ACTION: Let's prayerfully do self evaluation regarding the extent we are meeting the requirements for being servants of the Lord. Pray for mercy

_____

_____

**Today is August 13th, Day #226 in year 2024.
There are 140 days remaining in year 2024**

RESTORATION I

SCRIPTURE: *"And I will restore to you the years that the locust hath eaten, the cankerworm, and the caterpiller, and the palmerworm, my great army which I sent among you"* ***(Joel 2:25)***

PRAYER: Father, thank You for the power to restore belongs to You (e. g Lazarus; lost axe; etc)
please let there be quick restoration of all my lost blessings (financial, health, ideas, spiritual etc) stolen by the enemy. Oh Lord, for me and all persons connected with me, please seal the mouth of all cankerworm, the caterpiller, and the palmerworm, in Jesus name

ACTION: Let's us prayerfully *"..call those things which be not as though they were."* ***(Rom. 4:17b)***

_____
_____

**Today is August 14th, Day #227 in year 2024.
There are 139 days remaining in year 2024**

FAITH WITHOUT GOOD WORKS IS DEAD

SCRIPTURE: *"For as the body without the spirit is dead, so faith without works is dead also"* **(James 2:26)**

PRAYER: Father Your word declares *"This is a faithful saying, and these things I want you to affirm constantly, that those who have believed in God should be careful to maintain good works. These things are good and profitable to men."* **(Titus 3:8 NKJV)**. Almighty God, please increase my faith in You and give me the grace to do greater works for you to keep my faith alive in Jesus name

ACTION: Let us take delight in doing God's work prayerfully, *"..calling those things which be not as though they were."* **(Rom. 4:17b)**

**Today is August 15th, Day #228 in year 2024.
There are 138 days remaining in year 2024**

BLESSED FOR KEEPING THE WORDS OF THE BIBLE

SCRIPTURE: *"Behold, I am coming quickly! Blessed is he who keeps the words of the prophecy of this book." **(Rev. 22:7 NKJV)***

PRAYER: Father, Your word declares *"But be ye doers of the word, and not hearers only, deceiving your own selves."(James 1:22)*. Dear Lord, please give me the grace to be hearer and keeper of Your word such that whenever You return to take Your own I will be ready to be raptured in Jesus name

ACTION: Let us prayerfully remind ourselves and others daily that Jesus Christ will soon return

_____
_____

**Today is August 16th, Day #229 in year 2024.
There are 137 days remaining in year 2024**

SIN BREEDS SORROWS

SCRIPTURE: *"He who sows iniquity will reap sorrow, And the rod of his anger will fail."* ***(Pro. 22:8 NKJV)***

PRAYER: Father, Your word makes it clear that the soul that sins shall die *(Ezek 18:4, 20)*. Almighty God, please deliver us from sowing sins and reaping sorrows, shame and other losses

ACTION: Let us pray that sins shall not have dominion over us

_____

_____

**Today is August 17th, Day #230 in year 2024.
There are 136 days remaining in year 2024**

BLESSED FOR FEEDING THE POOR

SCRIPTURE: *"He who is generous will be blessed, For he gives some of his food to the poor"* ***(Proverbs 22:9 AMP)***

PRAYER: Father, Your word declares that *"He that giveth unto the poor shall not lack...."**(Proverbs 28:27)*. Dear Lord, as You are generous, please help us to be generous in giving to the poor and the needy and to be blessed according to Your word in *Pro 28:27*

ACTION: Let us prayerfully lend to the Lord by having pity on the poor *(Pro 19:17)*

_____

_____

**Today is August 18th, Day #231 in year 2024.
There are 135 days remaining in year 2024**

THE LORD REJECTS ELI'S HOUSEHOLD

SCRIPTURE: *"Therefore the Lord God of Israel says: 'I said indeed that your house and the house of your father would walk before Me forever.' But now the Lord says: 'Far be it from Me; for those who honor Me I will honor, and those who despise Me shall be lightly esteemed.'"*
(I Samuel 2:30 NKJV)

PRAYER: Father, please have mercy on me and don't let any member of my family do any abominable thing to You that will cause You to reject our family from walking before You (serving as a Minister in Your house) as You withdrew such a privilege from Eli's household due to the sinful lifestyle, worthlessness and waywardness of his children of which their father Eli failed to curtail and control
(1 Sam 1:12-17; 22-25)

ACTION: Let us prayerfully train up our children in the way of the Lord and as they grow old supervise them and continue to pray that they will not depart from the way of the Lord

_____

_____

**Today is August 19th, Day #232 in year 2024.
There are 134 days remaining in year 2024**

LETTING YOUR SHEPHERD BE THE LORD

SCRIPTURE: *"The Lord is my shepherd; I shall not want." (Psalms 23:1 NKJV)*

PRAYER: Father, thank You for Your Son Jesus Christ is the good Shepherd *(John 10:11, 14)*. Oh Lord, My Savior please continue to be my Shepherd as You were to David and let me also have testimonies like David and much more *(Psalm 23:1-6)*

ACTION: Having Jesus Christ as one's Shepherd calls for Salvation of that person's soul.
Let us pray for all those that are yet to be saved, that the power of the Good Shepherd will draw them to surrender their lives to Jesus Christ as their Lord and Savior

_____
_____

**Today is August 20th, Day #233 in year 2024.
There are 133 days remaining in year 2024**

DANIEL INTERPRETS THE KINGS DREAM

SCRIPTURE: *"This image's head was of fine gold, its chest and arms of silver, its belly and thighs of bronze," **(Dan. 2:32 NKJV)***

PRAYER: Father, Your word declares: *"...But there is a God in heaven who reveals secrets,..." **(Daniel 2:28 NKJV)*** Oh God in heaven, please give us insights and revelation knowledge akin to the one You gave Daniel that enabled him to know and interpret king Nebuchadnezzar's dream, an act that prevented Daniel, other wise men, the astrologers, the magicians, and soothsayers in the king's territory from been killed by the king's order for their inability to know and interpret the king's dream *(Dan 2:17-45)*

ACTION: Let us prayerfully claim God's promise in *Isaiah 45:3:* *"And I will give thee the treasures of darkness, and hidden riches of secret places, that thou mayest know that I, the LORD, which call thee by thy name, am the God of Israel"*

**Today is August 21st, Day #234 in year 2024.
There are 132 days remaining in year 2024**

THE LORD GOD THAT FIGHTS FOR HIS PROPLE

SCRIPTURE: *"You have seen all that the Lord your God has done to all these nations because of you, for the Lord your God is He who has fought for you."*
(Joshua 23:3 NKJV)

PRAYER: Father, Your word declares: *"The LORD is a man of war: the LORD is his name"* *(Exo. 15:3)*; and that *"The LORD shall fight for you, and ye shall hold your peace." (Exo. 14:14).*
Almighty God, by Your grace I am Your's; please fight all my battles for me and give me victory and peace as You did for the Israelites under the leadership of Moses *(Exo 14&15)*; Joshua *(Josh 23)*, Jehoshaphat and Judah *(2 Chron. 20)*

ACTION: For God to fight your battles of life you must belong to Him by surrendering your life to Him. If you have not, do so today and begin to enjoy peace from the Prince of Peace *(Matt 11:28, John 3:16; John 16:33)*

Today is August 22nd, Day #235 in year 2024. There are 131 days remaining in year 2024

FEARING NO EVIL DUE TO PRESENCE OF THE FATHER

SCRIPTURE: *"Yea, though I walk through the valley of the shadow of death, I will fear no evil; For You are with me; Your rod and Your staff, they comfort me." **(Psalms 23:4 NKJV)***

PRAYER: Father, Your word declares: *"....The beloved of the LORD shall dwell in safety by him; and the LORD shall cover him all the day long, and he shall dwell between his shoulders."-(Deuteronomy 33:12)*. Almighty God, no matter how many dangers, or afflictions we may face, please be with us as our shield and shelter and let us not fear for Your word declares that *"....God hath not given us the spirit of fear; but of power, and of love, and of a sound mind"* (2 Timothy 1:7)

ACTION: Let us prayerfully claim the scripture in *Isaiah 43:1-4*

_____

_____

**Today is August 23rd, Day #236 in year 2024.
There are 130 days remaining in year 2024**

BALAAM'S CURSE TURNED TO BLESSING

SCRIPTURE: *"But the Lord your God refused to listen to Balaam. Instead, he turned Balaam's curse into a blessing for you because the Lord your God loves you." **(Deut. 23:5 GW)***

PRAYER: Father, Your word declares: *"...the curse causeless shall not come." **(Pro.26:2b KJV)** and that: "...those who are believers in Christ Jesus can no longer be condemned."**(Romans 8:1 GW)**.* Oh Righteous God my Redeemer, from my foundation and throughout my life please turn every Balaam-like curse into blessings in Jesus name

ACTION: Let us praise God and claim His promise in *Isa 54:17*

_____

_____

Today is August 24th, Day #237 in year 2024, There are 129 days remaining in year 2024

MIRACLE OF TURNING ROCK TO WATER

SCRIPTURE: *"He turns a rock into a pool filled with water and turns flint into a spring flowing with water."* (Psalms 114:8 GW)

PRAYER: Father, Your word declares. *"For with God nothing shall be impossible."* ***(Luke 1:37)***
Please turn every scarce (but needful) resource in my life to surplus as You did for the Israelites in the wilderness when they lacked water and, through Moses, You turned a rock into a pool filled with water

ACTION: Plead the blood of Jesus on yourself and claim the scripture ***Psalms 107:35***: *"He turneth the wilderness into a standing water, and dry ground into watersprings."*

_____

_____

**Today is August 25th, Day #238 in year 2024.
There are 128 days remaining in year 2024**

ADHERING TO WORSHIPING GOD LIKE ANNA

SCRIPTURE: *"and she had been a widow for 84 years. Anna never left the temple courtyard but worshiped day and night by fasting and praying."* **(Luke 2:37 GW)**

PRAYER: Father, Your word declares: *"…Thou shalt worship the Lord thy God, and him only shalt thou serve"* **(Luke 4:8b)** and that we should *"…pray without ceasing"* **(1 Thes. 5:17)**
Dear Lord please increase my passion for Your Church and to worship and praise You more assiduously as did Prophetess Anna the widow **(Luke 2:36-38)**

ACTION: Regarding God's Church let us pray to have a mindset like Peter **(Matt 16:16-18)** and like King David **(Psalms 27:4)**

Today is August 26th, Day #239 in year 2024.
There are 127 days remaining in year 2024

HOLD FAST TO THE LORD GOD THE HIGHEST

SCRIPTURE: *"but you shall hold fast to the Lord your God, as you have done to this day." **(Joshua 23:8 NKJV)***

PRAYER: Father, You are my Lord and my God; please help me to hold fast to You (to Your word, worship, ordinances; and strict observation of them; and to have strong faith, affection, hope, trust, and confidence in You just as Moses and Joshua admonished the Israelites to do before and after they entered the Promised land *(Deut 13:4; Joshua 23:1-9)*

ACTION: Let us pray to perpetually abide in Jesus Christ as He abides in us so that we can be more fruitful and effective *(John 15:4-5)*

_____

_____

Today is August 27th, Day #240 in year 2024.
There are 126 days remaining in year 2024

FRIENDLY WITH FOREIGNER?

SCRIPTURE: *"You must not oppress foreigners. You know what it's like to be a foreigner, for you yourselves were once foreigners in the land of Egypt." (Exodus 23:9 NLT)*

PRAYER: Father, Your word declares, *"Be not forgetful to entertain strangers: for thereby some have entertained angels unawares" (Hebrews 13:2)*
Oh gracious God, help us to be kind and helpful to foreigners as part of observing 'the law of social justice' You laid down for the Israelites via Moses their leader *(Exo. 22:16-Exo 23:9)*

ACTION: Instead of oppressing and cheating foreigners, let us prayerfully seek God's guidance in knowing how be of help to foreigners.

_____

_____

Today is August 28th, Day #241 in year 2024.
There are 125 days remaining in year 2024

HELPING TO FURNISH GOD'S HOUSE

SCRIPTURE: *"Hiram also made ten bronze basins. Each basin held 240 gallons. Every basin was six feet wide. There was one basin on each of the ten stands." **(1 Kings 7:38 GW)***

PRAYER: Father, king Solomon built an elaborate and beautiful Temple for You and Hiram was a notable contributors in the furnishing of the Temple. Hiram made and donated 10 bronze basins (each holding 240 gallons of water for the use of the priests in their sacred office *(1 kings Chps 6;7; 2 Chron 4:6)*
Dear Lord, please bless me and empower me to be a major contributor to building and furnishing Your house as did Solomon and Hiram

ACTION: Let us pray for God to bless all who are providing support for building projects in various churches

_____
_____

**Today is August 29th, Day #242 in year 2024.
There are 124 days remaining in year 2024**

ENVY NOT AND STAY AWAY FROM EVIL MEN

SCRIPTURE: *"Do not be envious of evil men, Nor desire to be with them;"* ***(Proverbs 24:1 NKJV)***

PRAYER: Father, Your word declares *"Enter not into the path of the wicked, and go not in the way of evil men"* ***(Proverbs 4:14)***
Almighty God, please don't let me be envious of evil men nor be unequally yoked with them for, by Your grace, I am the light of the world and light has no communion with darkness ***(Matt 5:14; 2 Cor. 6:14)***

ACTION: Let us pray for God to order our steps away from anything that is evil

Today is August 30th, Day #243 in year 2024.
There are 123 days remaining in year 2024

WONDERFUL WORK OF GOD OF ESTABLISHING THE WORLD ON WATERS

SCRIPTURE: *"For He has founded it upon the seas And established it upon the waters." **(Psalms 24:2 NKJV)***

PRAYER: Father, thank You for Your amazing work of creation including establishing the entire world on waters without sinking!
Please Lord, keep this world in the peaceful order You created it to be and don't let Satan and his agents create chaos, calamities, and disruptions as he the goes up and down in the world *(Job 1:7)*

ACTION: Let us pray against pollution of the good world made by God

_____

_____

Today is August 31st, Day #244 in year 2024.
There are 122 days remaining in year 2024

CRITERIA FOR MAKING IT TO ABODE OF JESUS CHRIST?

SCRIPTURE: *"Who may ascend into the hill of the Lord? Or who may stand in His holy place?" **(Psalms 24:3 NKJV)***

PRAYER: Lord, Jesus, thank You for the place You have gone to prepare for me and for Your promise to come again, and receive me unto Yourself such that where You are, there will I be also **(John 14:3)**. Please Lord, help me to satisfy the criteria You have specified for being with You in Your abode, viz
*".....clean hands and a pure heart, Who has not lifted up his soul to an idol, Nor sworn deceitfully." **(Psalms 24:4 NKJV)***
We shall not fall short of these criteria in Jesus name.

ACTION: Let us prayerfully obey the injunction in **Heb 12:14** so that we can see and dwell with Jesus Christ forever

SEPTEMBER

Today is September 1st, Day #245 in the year 2024. There are 121 days remaining in year 2024.

SEEKING FOR WISDOM AND KNOWLEDGE FROM THE SAVIOR

SCRIPTURE: *"And by knowledge shall the chambers be filled with all precious and pleasant riches"*. ***(Proverbs 24:4)***

PRAYER: Father, your word declares, *"Through wisdom is an house builded; and by understanding it is established: 4 And by knowledge shall the chambers be filled with all precious and pleasant riches"* ***(Pro 24:4-5, KJV)***. Almighty God, please give me wisdom knowledge and understanding and everything I need to build up my life, my family, my house and anything I embark upon to glorify You in Jesus name

ACTION: Let us thank God for the new month of September and pray that He will give us wisdom and everything we need to live safely and successfully throughout of September and beyond in Jesus name

_____

_____

Today is September 2nd, Day #246 in year 2024. There are 120 days remaining in year 2024

DELIVERANCE FROM DECEIVERS

SCRIPTURE: *"For many will come in My name, saying, 'I am the Christ,' and will deceive many."* ***(Matthew 24:5 NKJV)***

PRAYER: Father, with respect to Signs of the end of Times, End of the Age, The Coming Back of Jesus Christ and other things, please deliver me from deceivers no matter how many and how tricky they may be. Please Lord, let me always remember what Your word says
"....that day and hour no one knows, not even the angels of heaven, but My Father only." ***(Matthew 24:36 NKJV).***

ACTION: Although we don't know the exact day of End of Age and Return of Jesus Christ let us pay keen attention to the signs provided for us in ***(Matt 24:36-44)***

_____

_____

**Today is September 3rd, Day #247 in year 2024.
There are 119 days remaining in year 2024**

COMING OUT AND RESTORED FROM CAPTIVITY

SCRIPTURE: *"For I will set My eyes on them for good, and I will bring them back to this land; I will build them and not pull them down, and I will plant them and not pluck them up." (Jeremiah 24:6 NKJV)*

PRAYER: Father, thank You, for Your plan for me is for good and not for evil *(Jer 29:11)*; in any way I have been swayed away from my destiny please set Your eyes on me for good, bring me back and restore me to be planted to my ordained destiny as You told Prophet Jeremiah You would do for Jeconiah and some Jews who were carried in to captivity in Babylon by Nebuchadnezzar *(Jeremiah 24:1-7)*

ACTION: Let us prayerfully claim the promise of God in *Joel 2:25-27*

**Today is September 4th Day #248 in year 2024.
There are 118 days remaining in year 2024**

CRYING TO THE COMPASSIONATE CHRIST

SCRIPTURE: *"So they cried out to the Lord; and He put darkness between you and the Egyptians, brought the sea upon them, and covered them. And your eyes saw what I did in Egypt. Then you dwelt in the wilderness a long time." (Joshua 24:7 NKJV).*

PRAYER: Father, thank You being a compassionate God. Please hear me, rescue me and meet me at the point of my need as You did to the Israelites who cried to You and You took them out of slavery in Egypt to the promised land; to Lazarus whom You brought back to life when his sisters cried to You *(John 11; 38-44)*; to The blind Bartimaeus whose eye sights You restored when he cried to You *(Mark 10:46-52)*; etc

ACTION: Let us praise the prayer answering and compassionate Lord

_____

_____

**Today is September 5th Day #249 in year 2024.
There are 117 days remaining in year 2024**

GATES MUST GIVE WAY FOR THE COMING IN OF THE KING OF GLORY

SCRIPTURE: *"Who is this King of glory? The Lord strong and mighty, The Lord mighty in battle." (Psalms 24:8 NKJV)*

PRAYER: Omnipotent God, in Your name, I command all 'gates' and 'everlasting doors' (potential obstacles and hindrances) to be lifted away so that You, Lord of hosts, the King of glory, who is strong and mighty in battle, can come into my life unhindered.

ACTION: Let us prayerfully rededicate our entire life and body unto God for His total control without any contention

_____
_____

Today is September 6th Day #250 in year 2024. There are 116 days remaining in year 2024

DANGER OF SPEAKING AGAINST GOD'S SERVANTS

SCRIPTURE: *"Remember what the Lord your God did to Miriam on the way when you came out of Egypt!" **(Deut. 24:9 NKJV)***

PRAYER: Father Your word declares, *"...Do not touch My anointed ones, And do My prophets no harm." **(Psalms 105:15 NKJV)**.* Please Lord, help me to bridle my tongue so as not to speak against or attack Your anointed servants as did Miriam who spoke against Moses and You punished her with leprosy and isolation for seven days ***(Num chap.12)***

ACTION: Instead of condemning servants of God, let us pray for them. If we found them in error pray to God for guidance as to how to deal with the error to effect correction without sinning

Today is September 7th Day #251 in year 2024.
There are 115 days remaining in year 2024

CRAVING TO UNDERSTAND JESUS CHRIST

SCRIPTURE: *"But they did not understand the statement which He spoke to them." **(Luke 2:50 NKJV)***

PRAYER: Lord Jesus, thank You for You are the Word (John 1:1) and Your word declares, *"... the words that I speak unto you, they are spirit, and they are life." **(John 6:63)***; and that *"...the Comforter, which is the Holy Ghost, whom the Father will send in my name, he shall teach you all things,...." **(John 14:26)***.
Oh Lord, with the help of the Holy Spirit please give me a thorough understanding of Your word and let it continue to be a lamp unto my feet and a light to my path in Jesus name ***(Ps119:105)***

ACTION: Let us pray that God by His grace will bless us with wisdom and understanding as He did for Solomon ***(1 Kings 4:29)***

_____
_____

Today is September 8th Day #252 in year 2024. There are 114 days remaining in year 2024

LIFTING UP OUR SOULS UNTO THE LORD

SCRIPTURE: *"To You, O Lord, I lift up my soul." **(Psalms 25:1 NKJV)***

PRAYER: Almighty God my Father, please favor me and let me always lift up my soul unto You to: receive help ***(Psa 33:20)***; receive healing ***(Psa 41:4)***; be delivered from death ***(Psa 33:19)***; for redemption ***(Psa 49:8)***; and for other blessings in Jesus name

ACTION: Let us pray that; as His servants; the Lord will rejoice our souls ***(Psalms 86:4)***

_____

_____

Today is September 9th Day #253 in year 2024. There are 113 days remaining in year 2024

CHRIST-LIKE CHILDREN

SCRIPTURE: *"And Jesus increased in wisdom and stature, and in favour with God and man"* **(Luke 2:52)**

PRAYER: Almighty God, please pattern the lives, growth and development of our Children after that of Jesus Christ *(Luke 2:52)*. Let our adults also go about doing good like Jesus Christ of Nazareth *(Acts 10:38)*

ACTION: Lets pray for God's wisdom in raising up our children

_____

_____

**Today is Sept 10th; Day #254 in year 2024.
There are 112 more days remaining in year 2024**

PETITION TO KILL PAUL

SCRIPTURE: *"They said to Festus, 'Please listen to us. We really want you to bring Paul here to Jerusalem. You can judge him here. Then we would be very happy.' They wanted to kill Paul while he was travelling to Jerusalem." **(Acts 25:3 EASY)***

PRAYER: Lord Jesus, thank You for Your promise that *"No weapon formed against me shall prosper, And every tongue which rises against me in judgment You shall condemn...." Isaiah 54:17 NKJV*; please Lord, let every plan of the evil ones to kill, to steal and to destroy us backfire on them in Jesus name

ACTION: Decree that any conspiracy to kill you will fail in Jesus' name

_____

_____

**Today is September 11th Day #255 in year 2024.
There are 111 days remaining in year 2024**

PRAYER FOR KNOWING GOD'S WAY AND PATH

SCRIPTURE: *"Show me Your ways, O Lord; Teach me Your paths." (Psalms 25:4 NKJV)*

PRAYER: Father, please show me Your ways and teach me Your paths according to Your word that says; *"....And many people shall go and say, Come ye, and let us go up to the mountain of the LORD, to the house of the God of Jacob; and he will teach us of his ways, and we will walk in his paths: ..."* **"Isaiah 2:3"**

ACTION: Let us prayerfully claim the scripture in ***Pro. 5:21***: *"For the ways of man are before the eyes of the Lord, And He ponders all his paths."*

_____

_____

Today is September 12th Day #256 in year 2024. There are 110 days remaining in year 2024

LED AND TAUGHT IN THE TRUTH OF THE LORD?

SCRIPTURE: *"Lead me in Your truth and teach me, For You are the God of my salvation; On You I wait all the day." (Psalm 25:5 NKJV)*

PRAYER: Father, thank You for You are: *"....the way, the truth, and the life: ...." (John 14:6)*; Please Lead me in Your truth and teach me Your ways in Jesus name.

ACTION: Let's pray that we'll never follow the way that seems right but ends in death in Jesus name *(Pro.14:12)*

Today is September 13th, Day #257 in year 2024. There are 109 days remaining in year 2024

LIVING A PROSPEROUS AND PEACEFUL LIFE

SCRIPTURE: *"And thus you shall say to him who lives in prosperity: 'Peace be to you, peace to your house, and peace to all that you have!"* ***(I Samuel 25:6 NKJV)***

PRAYER: Almighty God, please give me the grace to continue to obey You and serve You diligently so that I can spend my days in prosperity, and my years in pleasures. ***(Job 36:11)***. Lord, as You let me live in prosperity please encompass me and my household also with Your peace that passes all understanding in Jesus name.

ACTION: Let's us prayerfully claim the scripture in ***3 John 1:2***

Today is September 14th, Day #258 in year 2024. There are 108 days remaining in year 2024

FORGIVING YOUTH ERA SINS BY GOD THE FATHER

SCRIPTURE: *"Do not remember the sins of my youth, nor my transgressions; According to Your mercy remember me, For Your goodness' sake, O Lord." **(Psalms 25:7 NKJV)***

PRAYER: Almighty God, I thank and praise You for Your mercy and goodness sake, by which You have forgiven all my sins and transgressions since my youth era according to Your word that declares: *"For I will be merciful to their unrighteousness, and their sins and their iniquities will I remember no more"* **(Heb. 8:12)**

ACTION: Let's us prayerfully claim the scripture in *1 John 1:7b*: *"..the blood of Jesus Christ his Son cleanseth us from all sin"*

Today is September 15th, Day #259 in year 2024.
There are 107 days remaining in year 2024

GOOD AND UPRIGHT IS THE LORD GOD

SCRIPTURE: *"Good and upright is the Lord; Therefore He teaches sinners in the way."* ***(Psalms 25:8 NKJV)***

PRAYER: Father, thank You for being a "gracious, good, righteous, merciful and faithful God; please teach us to humbly walk before You and be perfect as You told Abraham to do in Jesus name *(Gen 17:1)*.

ACTION: Let's thank God for saving us and pray that He will use us to teach sinners in His way

_____

_____

Today is September 16th, Day #260 in year 2024. There are 106 days remaining in year 2024

PLAQUE TERMINATED DUE TO PHINEHAS' ACTION

SCRIPTURE: *"but those who died in the plague numbered 24,000." (Numbers 25:9 NIV)*

PRAYER: Father, by their sins, whoredom and idolatry character the nation of Israel provoked Your wrath and You released a plaque into their midst that killed 24,000 people in one day before Phinehas' zeal and Priestly action put an end to the killing by the ferocious plaque *(Num 25: 1-11)*. Oh Lord, have mercy on our nations, terminate all forms of sins, whoredom, idolatry and any unholy life styles that can provoke release of any form of plaque or disaster into our nations in Jesus name

ACTION: Let's us prayerfully covet Phinehas type of anointing that will honor the Lord, defend His cause and provoke peace in our communities and world in Jesus name.

_____

_____

**Today is September 17th, Day #261 in year 2024.
There are 105 days remaining in year 2024**

POWER OF PROPHECY

SCRIPTURE: *"And I will grant the power of prophecy to My two witnesses for 1,260 (42 months; three and one-half years), dressed in sackcloth." (Revelation 11:3 AMPC)*

PRAYER: Father, Your word declares, *"But you shall receive power (ability, efficiency, and might) when the Holy Spirit has come upon you, and you shall be My witnesses in Jerusalem and all Judea and Samaria and to the ends (the very bounds) of the earth." (Acts 1:8 AMPC)*. Please, Lord empower us to be faithful witnesses to You as did those two witnesses mentioned in *Rev 11:3*, who possibly are Moses and Elijah

ACTION: Let's prayerfully obey the assignment given to us as believers in *Mark 16:15*

Today is Sept 18th; Day #262 in the year 2024. There are 104 days remaining in year 2024.

SINGING 'OUR CITY IS STRONG

SCRIPTURE: *"In that day, everyone in the land of Judah will sing this song: Our city is strong! We are surrounded by the walls of God's salvation."* **(Isa. 26:1 NLT)**

PRAYER: Father, Your word declares, *"Righteousness exalts a nation, But sin is a reproach to any people."* **(Pro14:34 NKJV).**
Oh Lord, let more people be saved and live righteously in our cities to provoke joyful songs of strength in our land *(Neh 8:10b)*

ACTION: Pray that Godly agenda will prevail in most cities of the world to make them strong in the LORD.

_____

_____

**Today is September 19th, Day #263 in year 2024.
There are 103 days remaining in year 2024**

LIVING WHERE SHOWN BY THE LORD

SCRIPTURE: *"The Lord appeared to Isaac. He said, 'Do not go to Egypt. Instead, live in the land that I will show to you."* **(Gen. 26:2, EASY)**

PRAYER: Father, Your word declares, *"I will instruct thee and teach thee in the way which thou shalt go: I will guide thee with mine eye"* **(Psalms 32:8)**
Almighty God please instruct, guide, direct, show and lead me where to go; please don't let me go to 'Egypt' or any place You do not approve for me to go in Jesus name

ACTION: Let us prayerfully claim God's word in **Psalm 37:23**

_____

_____

Today is September 20th, Day #264 in year 2024.
There are 102 days remaining in year 2024

DWELLING IN BLESSED LAND WITH DESCENDANTS

SCRIPTURE: *"Dwell in this land, and I will be with you and bless you; for to you and your descendants I give all these lands, and I will perform the oath which I swore to Abraham your father."* ***(Genesis 26:3 NKJV)***

PRAYER: Father, Your word declares *"Every place that the sole of your foot shall tread upon, that have I given unto you, as I said unto Moses"* ***(Josh 1:3)***. Oh Lord, wherever You lead me to stay, please bless me there and my descendants and let us dwell there peacefully in Jesus name

ACTION: Let us prayerfully claim God's word in ***GEN 22:17***

_____

_____

**Today is September 21st, Day #265 in year 2024.
There are 101 days remaining in year 2024**

AVOIDING FOOLISH ARGUMENTS

SCRIPTURE: *"Don't answer the foolish arguments of fools, or you will become as foolish as they are."* **(Proverbs 26:4 NLT)**

PRAYER: Father, Your word declares *"....The fool hath said in his heart, There is no God. Corrupt are they, and have done abominable iniquity: there is none that doeth good." (Pro:53:1)*. Oh Lord, please teach and direct me when and how to avoid ungodly arguments with fools and unbelievers in Jesus name

ACTION: Let us prayerfully obey the instructions in *2 Cor 6:14)*

_____

_____

Today is September 22nd, Day #266 in year 2024.
There are 100 days remaining in year 2024

SEEKING GOD ATTRACTS SUCCESSES

SCRIPTURE: *"Uzziah sought God during the days of Zechariah, who taught him to fear God. And as long as the king sought guidance from the Lord, God gave him success." (2 Chronicles 26:5 NLT)*

PRAYER: Father, please give me the grace to seek and serve you diligently and be guided by You in everything I do so that I will prosper *(2 Chro. 15:15)*, not lack any good thing *(Psa 34:10)* and receive great and glorious successes from God as it happened to Uzziah, David, Joseph, Paul, etc

PRAYER: Father, Your word declares *"....The fool hath said in his heart, There is no God. Corrupt are they, and have done abominable iniquity: there is none that doeth good." (Pro:53:1)*. Oh Lord, please teach and direct me when and how to avoid ungodly arguments with fools and unbelievers in Jesus name

ACTION: Let us pray daily to have the faith to please and seek God diligently to be rewarded by Him *(Heb 11:6)*

_____

_____

Today is September 23rd, Day #267 in year 2024. There are 99 days remaining in year 2024

PERSECUTION BY TRIAL FOR HOPING IN GOD'S PROMISE

SCRIPTURE: *"Now I am on trial because of my hope in the fulfillment of God's promise made to our ancestors." (Acts of the Apostles 26:6 NLT)*

PRAYER: Father, Your word declares *"Yea, and all that will live godly in Christ Jesus shall suffer persecution". (2 Tim.3:12)*
Almighty God, if by chance I face any persecution as a result of my hope in the fulfillment of Your promises about me and my ancestors, please give me the grace to prevail as You did for Paul, Jeremiah, etc

ACTION: Let us be determined that nothing, including persecution shall separate us from the love of God *(Rom 8:35)*

_____

_____

Today is September 24th, Day #268 in year 2024. There are 98 days remaining in year 2024

BLESSINGS OF OBEDIENCE I

SCRIPTURE: *"You will chase your enemies, and they shall fall by the sword before you." **(Leviticus 26:7 NKJV)***

PRAYER: Father thank You for promising various types of blessings that will accrue to anyone who obeys Your commandments and statues ***(Deut 28:1-2; Lev:1-13)***. Please Lord let all my enemies be chased and feel before me until they crash and fall woefully by the sword of the Lord in Jesus name

ACTION: Let us prayerfully claim God's promise in ***Deut 28:7***

_____

_____

Today is September 25th, Day #269 in year 2024. There are 97 days remaining in year 2024

LEANING ON THE MIGHTY AND EVERLASTING ARMS OF THE LORD

SCRIPTURE: *"So the Lord brought us out of Egypt with a mighty hand and with an outstretched arm, with great terror and with signs and wonders." **(Deuteronomy 26:8 NKJV)***

PRAYER: Father, with Your mighty hand, outstretched and everlasting arms please thrust out my enemies, set me free and bring me out of anything that amounts to 'Egypt' that has held me enslaved, bound, captive, incapacitated (e.g. sickness, poverty, stagnation, etc); just as You liberated the Israelites from Egypt

ACTION: Let us prayerfully claim God's promise in ***Deut 28:7***

Today is Sept 26th; Day #270 in year 2024.
There are 96 days remaining in year 2024

SANCTIFIED VERSUS SINFUL SOUL

SCRIPTURE: *"Do not gather my soul with sinners, Nor my life with bloodthirsty men," **(Psalms 26:9 NKJV)**.*

PRAYER: Father, Your word admonishes us not to be unequally yoked with unbelievers *(2 Cor. 6:14)*; please Lord help me to live sanctified and holy till the end so that my soul will not be gathered with those of bloodthirsty men and sinners in Jesus name

ACTION: Pray not to be a victim of wicked, sinful and bloodthirsty people

_____
_____

**Today is Sept 27th; Day #271 in the year 2024.
There are 95 days remaining in year 2024.**

CONTRIBUTIONS FOR BUILDING CHRIST'S CHURCH

SCRIPTURE: *"Many of the people contributed to help pay the cost of restoring the Temple: The governor 270 ounces of gold..." (Neh. 7: 70-72, GNT)*

PRAYER: Father, thank You for Your word that says, *"....give to Caesar what belongs to Caesar, and give to God what belongs to God" (Mk 12:17 NLT)*. Lord Jesus, please empower me such that I'll be able to contribute generously towards building and/or supporting Your Church as did the governor and his people during the restoration of the Temple in Jerusalem *(Neh. 7:70)*

ACTION: Give to beautify Christ's Church as you want Him to beautify your life as His 'Temple' *(1 Cor 6:19)*

_____

_____

Today is Sept 28th; Day #272 in year 2024.
There are 94 days remaining in year 2024

LORD IS MY SALVATION STRENGTH AND LIGHT

SCRIPTURE: *"The Lord is my light and my salvation; Whom shall I fear? The Lord is the strength of my life; Of whom shall I be afraid?"* **(Psa. 27:1 NKJV)**

PRAYER: Father, by Your grace I shall not fear or be afraid of any one because as You were to David, *"You are my rock and my fortress and my deliverer; The God of my strength, in whom I will trust; My shield and the horn of my salvation, My stronghold and my refuge; My Savior, You save me from violence."* **(II Samuel 22:2-3 NKJV)**. Dear Lord, may Your praise never depart from my mouth in Jesus name.

ACTION: Boldly declare, I put my Faith in God and I have nothing to fear in Jesus name.

_____

_____

Today is Sept 29th; Day #273 in year 2024. There are 93 days remaining in year 2024

DOING FATHER'S DESIRE

SCRIPTURE: *"Now therefore, please take your weapons, your quiver and your bow, and go out to the field and hunt game for me." **(Genesis 27:3 NKJV)***

PRAYER: Father, whatever You and/or my earthly / spiritual fathers and other bona fide leaders demand of me to do, please give me the grace to obey and do the father's will as did Esau to his father Isaac

ACTION: Pray to always Honor both your Heavenly and Earthly Fathers by doing their will

_____
_____

Today is Sept 30th; Day #274 in year 2024. There are 92 days remaining in year 2024

JUDAS' BETRAYAL OF JESUS

SCRIPTURE: *"Then Judas, His betrayer, seeing that He had been condemned, was remorseful and brought back the thirty pieces of silver to the chief priests and elders," (Matthew 27:3 NKJV)*

PRAYER: Father, Your word says *".....woe to that man by whom the Son of man is betrayed"(Mark 14:21).* Judas Iscariot betrayed Jesus and brought curse on himself that led him to commit suicide *(Matt 27:3-7).* Oh Lord please don't let me ever betray You.

ACTION: Let's give thanks to God for His mercy that endureth for ever *(Psa 118:29)*

_____
_____

OCTOBER

Today is October 1st Day #275 in year 2024. There are 91 more days remaining in year 2024

LIKE TO LIVE FOREVER IN THE HOUSE OF THE LORD?

SCRIPTURE: *"One thing I have desired of the Lord, that will I seek: That I may dwell in the house of the Lord All the days of my life, To behold the beauty of the Lord, And to inquire in His temple." **(Psalms 27:4 NKJV)***

PRAYER: Father, thank You for Your promise that says *"....In My Father's house are many mansions; if it were not so, I would have told you. I go to prepare a place for you. And if I go and prepare a place for you, I will come again and receive you to Myself; that where I am, there you may be also." (John 14:1-3 NKJV)*. Dear Lord, please give me the grace to spend eternity with You and dwell in the house. You have prepared for me in Your mansions *(John 14:1-3)*

ACTION: Let's us pray that when Jesus returns to take His own we shall be ready to be raptured with Him

Today is October 2nd Day #276 in year 2024. There are 90 days remaining in year 2024

SAFETY IN GOD'S SANCTUARY

SCRIPTURE: *"For he will conceal me there when troubles come; he will hide me in his sanctuary. He will place me out of reach on a high rock."* ***(Psalms 27:5 NLT)***

PRAYER: Father, thank you for Your promise that the gates of hell shall not prevail against Your Church ***(Mt 16:18)***. Oh Lord please let Your sanctuary all over the world continue to be a haven of safety and peace that is out of reach by Satan and his agents. Deliver us from all troubles in Jesus name

ACTION: Let's us pray and claim the scripture in ***Gal. 6:17***

Today is Oct. 3rd, Day #277, in year 2024.
There are 89 days remaining in year 2024.

FILLING THE WORLD WITH FRUIT

SCRIPTURE: *"In times to come Jacob will take root. Israel will blossom, bud, and fill the whole world with fruit." **(Isa. 27:6 GW)***

PRAYER: Father, as per Your word let us be fruitful and multiply and replenish the earth *(Gen 1:28)*; in particular, please give each member of Your Church the grace to be grounded in Christ and abound in good works including winning multitude of souls to fill the whole world for You in Jesus name.

ACTION: Let us pray that our lives will not reflect that of the plant described in *Luke 13:6*

_____

_____

Today is Oct 4th; Day #278 in year 2024.
There are 88 days remaining in year 2024

HEAR ME LORD WHEN I CALL FOR HELP

SCRIPTURE: *"Lord, hear me when I call to you for help. Be kind to me and answer me." **(Psa 27:7 EASY)***

PRAYER: Father Your word declares, *"'Call to Me, and I will answer you, and show you great and mighty things, which you do not know.'" **(Jer. 33:3 NKJV)***. Oh Lord, please empower me to pray unto You more fervently for help and let great and mighty things continue manifest in all areas of my life in Jesus name.

ACTION: Let us pray and claim God's promise for help in ***Isaiah (41:13)***

_____

_____

Today is Oct 5th; Day #279 in year 2024
There are 87 days remaining in year 2024

HOPELESS ARE PEOPLE WHO DIE WITHOUT HAVING GOD

SCRIPTURE: *"What hope do people without God have when it is time to die, when God takes their life away?." **(Job 27:8 EASY)***

PRAYER: Father, please let all those who have not given their lives to You do so before they die so that they can be hopeful of going to heaven. *(John 14:2)*

ACTION: Let's pray to never forsake the God we know so as not to miss our mansion in heaven *(John 14:2)*

_____

_____

Today is Oct 6th; Day #280 in year 2024.
There are 86 days remaining in year 2024

WHO DO YOU BELONG TO?

SCRIPTURE: *"Then Moses and the priests, the Levites, spoke to all Israel, saying, "Take heed and listen, O Israel: This day you have become the people of the Lord your God." (Deut. 27:9 NKJV)*

PRAYER: Father, thank You for Your word declares, *"But now, thus says the Lord, who created you, O Jacob, And He who formed you, O Israel: "Fear not, for I have redeemed you; I have called you by your name; You are Mine." (Isaiah 43:1 NKJV).* By Your grace, Oh Lord God, I belong to You for I have accepted You and surrendered my life to You as my Savior and You have redeemed me *(Rom 10:9-10, Eph. 2:8)*. Please Lord, by Your mercy let all those who have not given their lives to You hear about the gospel of Salvation through Jesus Christ and surrender their lives to Him so they can become people of the Lord God *(John 1:12, NKJV)*

ACTION: Let us pray for more wisdom from God to win souls unto Him *(Pro 11:30)*

_____

_____

**Today is Oct 7th; Day #281 in year 2024.
There are 85 days remaining in year 2024**

DIVINE EMPOWERMENT

SCRIPTURE: *"Jehoshaphat became more and more powerful. ....He had a big army of strong, brave soldiers in Jerusalem. These are the groups of the soldiers in each clan: From Judah's tribe, the officer who led the soldiers was Adnah. He had authority over 300,000 soldiers, in groups of 1,000. The next officer was Jehohanan. He had authority over 280,000 soldiers." (2 Chronicles 17:12-15 EASY)*

PRAYER: Father, please give me the grace to live a life pleasing unto You and to be empowered like king Jehoshaphat of Judah whom Your word declares, *"The Lord was with Jehoshaphat, who lived in the old way like his ancestor David. Jehoshaphat didn't dedicate his life to serving other gods—the Baals. So the Lord established Jehoshaphat's power over the kingdom. All the people of Judah gave gifts to Jehoshaphat, and he had a lot of riches and honor." (2 Chronicles 17:3, 5)*

ACTION: If you live to please God He will cause people to please You

_____

_____

Today is Oct 8th; Day #282 in year 2024.
There are 84 days remaining in year 2024

SAFE ARRIVAL AT SHORE

SCRIPTURE: *"Once we were safe on shore, we learned that we were on the island of Malta." **(Acts. 28:1 NLT)***

PRAYER: Father, in all our journeys, please grant us safety from origin to destination as You did for Apostle Paul and other 275 members of his entourage as they sailed safely to the island of Melita despite arduous circumstances like extreme cold, hunger, life threatening storms, poor navigation, shipwreck, etc *(Acts 27)*.

ACTION: let us pray that God's presence will go with us in all our trips in Jesus' name

**Today is Oct 9th; Day #283 in year 2024.
There are 83 days remaining in year 2024**

ROLLING AWAY RESTRICTIONS

SCRIPTURE: *"Suddenly, there was a powerful earthquake. An angel of the Lord had come down from heaven, rolled the stone away, and was sitting on it."* ***(Matt. 28:2 GW).***

PRAYER: Father, as You sent an Angel to roll away the rock that sealed the tomb of Jesus, please roll away every obstacle positioned to restrict my rising, promotion and fulfillment of destiny in Jesus name.

ACTION: Let us pray for removal of all road blocks along our paths of progress ***(Isaiah 57:14)***

_____

_____

Today is Oct 10th; Day #284 in year 2024. There are 82 days remaining in year 2024

DECEIT OF THE DRUNKARD

SCRIPTURE: *"The drunk people of Samaria think that their city is great. But their enemies will knock it down and walk all over it." (Isaiah 28:3 EASY)*

PRAYER: Father, Your word says drunkards are among those who will not inherit the kingdom of heaven *(1 Cor. 6:10)*. Dear Lord that sets the captive free; please deliver the drunkards from the spirit of drunkenness and deceit. Please give us the grace not to be drunk with wine; but to be filled with the Spirit *(Ephesians 5:18)*

ACTION: Abstain from wine and new wine which the Bible says can take away understanding, especially when used with whoredom *(Hosea 4:11)*

Today is Oct 11th; Day #285 in year 2024. There are 81 days remaining in year 2024

BOUNDLESS BLESSINGS

SCRIPTURE: *"Blessed shall be the fruit of your body, the produce of your ground and the increase of your herds, the increase of your cattle and the offspring of your flocks* **(Deut. 28:4 NKJV).**

PRAYER: Father, please give us the grace to diligently obey Your voice and carefully observe all Your commandments that will position us to enjoy boundless blessings in terms of fruitfulness and other life-enhancing benefits in Jesus name.

ACTION: Prayerfully claim the promise in *Psa 23:5*

Today is Oct 12th; Day #286 in year 2024.
There are 80 days remaining in year 2024

SHAKE OFF THE SNAKE

SCRIPTURE: *"Paul shook the snake into the fire and wasn't harmed." (Acts 28:5 GW)*

PRAYER: Father, Your word declares, *"And these signs shall follow them that believe; In my name shall they cast out devils;….They shall take up serpents; and …….it shall not hurt them; ……" (Mark 16:17-18)*. Lord Jesus, as that poisonous snake attached itself to Paul's hand but was unable to harm him and Paul shook it off into fire *(Acts 28: 3-5)*, please let every spiritual or physical 'snake' intending to attach itself to me be shaken off into fire, in Jesus name.

ACTION: Prayerfully claim the promise in *Luke 10:19*

_____

_____

Today is Oct 13th; Day #287 in year 2024. There are 79 days remaining in year 2024

PRAISE GOD FOR ANSWERED PRAYER

SCRIPTURE: *"Blessed be the Lord, Because He has heard the voice of my supplications!" **(Psalms 28:6 NKJV)***

PRAYER: Father, Your word declares, *"You faithfully answer our prayers with awesome deeds, O God our savior. You are the hope of everyone on earth, even those who sail on distant seas." **(Psalms 65:5 NLT)**.* I just want to thank You and praise You for all my prayers You have answered and will continue to answer. Dear Lord, please don't let Your praise ever depart from my mouth *(Psa 34:1-3)*.

ACTION: Let us Prayerfully claim the promise in ***Psalm 67: 5-7***

Today is Oct 14th; Day #288 in year 2024.
There are 78 days remaining in year 2024

DIVINE DEFENCE AGAINST ENEMIES AND ALL AGENTS OF THE DEVIL

SCRIPTURE: *"The Lord will conquer your enemies when they attack you. They will attack you from one direction, but they will scatter from you in seven!" **(Deuteronomy 28:7 NLT)***

PRAYER: Father, Your word tells us not to fear that the LORD God shall fight for us *(Deut. 3:22)*. Oh Lord, when our enemies and foes attack us please fight and scatter them and let them stumble and fall woefully in Jesus name *(Psalms 27:2 NLT)*

ACTION: As God did for Joshua, Israel and people of Gibeon, let us pray for God to send hailstones from heaven to destroy all our unrelenting enemies and attackers planning to us *(Josh 10:8-11)*

**Today is Oct 15th; Day #289 in year 2024.
There are 77 days remaining in year 2024**

SKILLED TEMPLE SINGERS AND GOD'S MUSICIANS

SCRIPTURE: *"All these Levites sang at the Lord's temple under the direction of their fathers Asaph, Jeduthun, and Heman. They played cymbals, lyres, and harps for worship in God's temple under the direction of the king. They, along with their relatives, were trained, skilled musicians for the Lord. There were 288 of them."* **(1 Chronicles 25:6-7 GW)**

PRAYER: Father, Your word enjoins us to serve You with gladness and singing **(Psalm 100:2 KJV)**; thank You for all genuine choir members in various congregations; please LORD, help us upgrade the tempo of our praise and worship in all Churches by adding to us skilled singers and trained instrumentalists like the 288 Levites described in today's lead scripture as "musicians for the Lord".

ACTION: Let us praise God with our voices and with the best musical instrument we can get

_____

_____

Today is Oct 16th; Day #290 in year 2024.
There are 76 days remaining in year 2024

SERVING AND SEEKING GOD WHO SEARCHES THE HEART

SCRIPTURE: *"As for you, my son Solomon, know the God of your father, and serve Him with a loyal heart and with a willing mind; for the Lord searches all hearts and understands all the intent of the thoughts. If you seek Him, He will be found by you; but if you forsake Him, He will cast you off forever." (I Chronicles 28:9 NKJV)*

PRAYER: Oh God that searches the heart, please let us serve and seek You with a loyal heart and a willing mind together with our family members. May we always find You and never forsake You so that we'll never be cast away from You forever

ACTION: God is a good rewarder, let us serve Him wholeheartedly as Paul suggests *Eph.(6:7-9)*

_____

_____

**Today is Oct 17th; Day #291 in year 2024.
There are 75 days remaining in year 2024**

CARING FOR FAMILY MEMBERS

SCRIPTURE: *"Joseph sent for his father Jacob and his relatives, 75 people in all." (Acts 7:14 GW)*

PRAYER: Father, thank You for teaching us in Your word *"....to love one another." (1 Thes. 4:9)*; to let brotherly continue *(Heb. 13:1)* and *"not to render evil for evil; but ever follow that which is good, both among yourselves, and to all men." (1 Thes. 5:15)*. Please Lord, give us the grace to have Joseph's type of caring attitude for our family members instead of repaying evil for evil. Dear Lord, in the remaining 75 days in year 2022 please do something glorious in our families in Jesus name.

ACTION: Let us prayerfully obey the injunction to honor our parents *(Eph 6: 2)* and to be our brother's keeper *(Gen. 4:9-10, Rom. 12:10; Pet 3:8)*

_____

_____

Today is Oct 18th; Day #292 in year 2024. There are 74 days remaining in year 2024

RIGHT ATTITUDE TOWARDS REBUKE

SCRIPTURE: *"He who is often rebuked, and hardens his neck, Will suddenly be destroyed, and that without remedy." (Proverbs 29:1 NKJV)*

PRAYER: Father, Your word declares, that, *"Open rebuke is better than secret love"* **(Proverbs 27:5 KJV)**; please Lord, give us the grace and wisdom to have the right attitude that will turn every rebuke directed towards us to profitable rewards for us in Jesus name

ACTION: In dealing rebuke let us remember and reflect on the fact that God said, *"Those whom I love I rebuke and discipline. So be earnest and repent"* **(Rev. 3:19)**

Today is Oct 19th; Day #293 in year 2024. There are 73 days remaining in year 2024

GODLY VERSUS WICKED LEADERS

SCRIPTURE: *"When the righteous are in authority, the people rejoice; But when a wicked man rules, the people groan." (Proverbs 29:2 NKJV)*

PRAYER: Father, please give us leaders who fear You and are competent and passionate in planning programs and projects that will make life better, safe and secured for the citizens they will rule over. By Your divine power oh Lord, please terminate the tenure of all existing and aspiring wicked, selfish, greedy, corrupt and incompetent leaders who are causing citizens of their domains to groan, moan, suffer hunger, poverty, untold hardship and often die prematurely. Almighty God, let power change hands so that Your good plans will materialize for the betterment of all the people You created in Your own image *(Jer 29:11)*

ACTION: Pray that righteous people will rule so that those they rule over will rejoice *(Pro.29:2)*

_____

_____

Today is Oct 20th; Day #294 in year 2024.
There are 72 days remaining in year 2024

DEVOTING TO GOD'S TEMPLE LIKE DAVID

SCRIPTURE: *"And now, because of my devotion to the Temple of my God, I am giving all of my own private treasures of gold and silver to help in the construction. This is in addition to the building materials I have already collected for his holy Temple." **(1 Chronicles 29:3 NLT)***

PRAYER: Father, please help and empower us to be zealous, and devoted to building and supporting Your Church as king David did, not only in terms of giving all his private treasures of gold, silver and other material for Temple construction, but also by his passion, presence and worship in the Temple as indicative in one of his declarations: *"One thing have I desired of the LORD, that will I seek after; That I may dwell in the house of the LORD all the days of my life, To behold the beauty of the LORD, and to enquire in his temple." **(Psalm 27:4 KJV)***.

ACTION: Let us prayerfully allow our devotion to God's physical Temple be driven by how devoted we are to our body which is also "God's Temple " ***(1 Cor 6:19)***

_____

_____

Today is Oct 21st; Day #295 in year 2024.
There are 71 days remaining in year 2024

GREAT AND MAJESTIC IS VOICE OF GOD.

SCRIPTURE: *"The voice of the Lord is powerful; the voice of the Lord is majestic." **(Psa. 29:4 NLT)***

PRAYER: Father, Your word declares: *"When God spoke from Mount Sinai his voice shook the earth, but now he makes another promise: "Once again I will shake not only the earth but the heavens also."* **(Hebrews 12:26 NLT)**. Lord Jesus how majestic and sweet is Your voice! whenever You descend from heaven with a shout, with the voice of an archangel to take Your own with You to heaven and with the trumpet of God, please let me be ready to be rapturable in Jesus name **(I Thess. 4:16-17 NKJV)**

ACTION: Let us speak, praise and honor the Lord for His majesty.

Today is Oct 22nd; Day #296 in year 2024.
There are 70 days remaining in year 2024

FORSAKING FLATTERY

SCRIPTURE: *"A man who flatters his neighbor spreads a net for his own feet." **(Pro 29:5 AMPC)***

PRAYER: Father, Your word declares: *"The LORD shall cut off all flattering lips, and the tongue that speaketh proud things:" **(Psalms 12:3 KJV)***. Dear LORD, please don't let me be the object or subject of flattery and/or proud words in Jesus name

ACTION: Determine never to be a Flatterer so as not to spread a net for your own feet

_____
_____

Today is Oct 23rd; Day #297 in year 2024.
There are 69 days remaining in year 2024

EVIL PEOPLE VERSUS GOOD PEOPLE

SCRIPTURE: *"Evil people are defeated by their sin, but good people will sing and be happy."* ***(Proverbs 29:6 ERV)***

PRAYER: Father, thank You because, by Your grace, I am connected with You and I am a good person; please let goodness and mercy follow me all the days of my life that I may sing and be happy always. Oh Lord of mercy, please let all evil people depart from their evil ways and run to You, in Jesus name.

ACTION: You were created to be good *(Gen 1:)* therefore decide to be a good person

_____

_____

Today is Oct 24th; Day #298 in year 2024. There are 68 days remaining in year 2024

PRAYING FOR PEACE TO HAVE PEACE

SCRIPTURE: *"And seek the peace of the city where I have caused you to be carried away captive, and pray to the Lord for it; for in its peace you will have peace." (Jeremiah 29:7 NKJV)*

PRAYER: Lord Jesus, thank You for You are the Prince of Peace *(Isaiah 9:6)*; please let Your peace prevail in all the cities and and nations You have located us. By Your power Oh God we command all natural disasters such as floods, Dam failure, earthquake, hurricane, storms, Tsunami, cyclones, wildfire, droughts, heavy snow, volcanic eruptions, etc from manifesting wherever we are in Jesus name

ACTION: Pray daily to the Prince of Peace for peace in the world

Today is Oct 25th; Day #299 in year 2024. There are 67 days remaining in year 2024

DON'T BE DECEIVED

SCRIPTURE: *"For thus says the Lord of hosts, the God of Israel: Do not let your prophets and your diviners who are in your midst deceive you, nor listen to your dreams which you cause to be dreamed." (Jer. 29:8 NKJV)*

PRAYER: Father, Your word declares, *"...Take heed that ye be not deceived: for many shall come in my name, saying, I am Christ,....." (Luke 21)* and that, we *"..believe not every spirit, but try the spirits whether they are of God: because many false prophets are gone out into the world." (1 John 4:1)*. Almighty God, please don't let us be victims of deceivers, false prophets, diviners and evil dreams in Jesus name.

ACTION: Determine to not deceive any one so that no one will deceive you *(Gal 6:7)*

_____

_____

Today is Oct 26th; Day #300 in year 2024. There are 66 days remaining in year 2024

GOD'S WRATH ON FORSAKERS OF HIM

SCRIPTURE: *"For indeed, because of this our fathers have fallen by the sword; and our sons, our daughters, and our wives are in captivity."* ***(II Chron 29:9 NKJV)***

PRAYER: Father, please don't let us ever forsake You and Your Church as did the Fathers of Judah and Jerusalem for which they faced Your sword and had their children taken into captivity ***(II Chron 28&29)***.

ACTION: Let us pray and determine never to foresake God

_____

_____

Today is Wednesday, Oct. 27th, Day #301 in year 2024. There are 65 days remaining in year 2024.

CHASING THE ENEMY UNTIL CRUSHED

SCRIPTURE: *"Gideon then crossed the Jordan River with his 300 men, and though exhausted, they continued to chase the enemy." (Judges 8:4 NLT)*

PRAYER: Father, please empower me to resist the devil unabated and to fight all my unrelenting enemies until they are crushed as Gideon and his warriors persistently crushed their enemies even though those enemies numbered about 5 times more than that of Gideon's *(Judges 8)*

ACTION: Following the Psalmist's example, let's look up to God for help to crush our enemies *(Psa 121:1)*

_____

_____

Today is Oct 28th; Day #302 in year 2024.
There are 64 days remaining in year 2024

LIFTED UP BY THE LORD

SCRIPTURE: *"I will extol You, O Lord, for You have lifted me up, And have not let my foes rejoice over me."* **(Psalms 30:1 NKJV)**

PRAYER: Father, I thank and extol You for You have lifted me up above sin, sorrow and my enemies. Oh Lord, by Your grace, please continue to lift me up higher and higher to embarrass all my foes and putting them to shame instead of them to be rejoicing over me and laughing me to stock, in Jesus' name.

ACTION: Let us praise and give thanks to God who is the Lifter of our heads *(Psa 3:3)*

Today is Oct 29th; Day #303 in year 2024. There are 63 days remaining in year 2024

CRYING TO GOD FOR CURE

SCRIPTURE: *"O Lord my God, I cried out to You, And You healed me." **(Psalms 30:2 NKJV)***

PRAYER: Father, Your word declares, *"For I will restore health unto thee, and I will heal thee of thy wounds, saith the LORD;..."**(Jer. 30:17)***. As Moses cried to You on behalf of Miriam and You healed her of her leprosy **(Num Chp.12)** and as the Blind Bartimaeus, cried to You, and You healed him of blindness **(Mark 10: 46-52)**, we cry to You, oh LORD to uproot anything You have not planted in our body and cure us of all ailments in Jesus name

ACTION: Let us Praise the God that declares *".. For I am the Lord who heals you." **(EXO 15:26)***

Today is Oct 30th; Day #304 in year 2024.
There are 62 days remaining in year 2024

REQUIREMENTS FOR RESTORATION

SCRIPTURE: *"he will restore your fortunes. He will have mercy on you and gather you from all the nations of the world where he will scatter you."* ***(Deut.30:3 GW)***

PRAYER: Father, through Moses You promised restoration to the Israelites on the following criteria: returning to You together with their children and obeying all Your commandments with all their heart and with all their soul, ***(Deut. 30:2-3, GW)***. Please Lord, empower and enable me and my household to remain connected and committed to You and to totally obey You so that we can enjoy all round divine restoration from You in the mighty name of Jesus

ACTION: Let us pray that our total reliance should be in God for total restoration

_____

_____

**Today is Oct 31st ; Day #305 in year 2024.
There are 61 days remaining in year 2024**

SING PRAISES TO GOD OH SAINTS

SCRIPTURE: *"Sing praise to the Lord, you saints of His, And give thanks at the remembrance of His holy name."* **(Psa 30:4 NKJV)**

PRAYER: Father, Your word declares, *"Praise the Lord! Sing to the Lord a new song, And His praise in the assembly of saints."* **(Psalms 149:1 NKJV).** Oh LORD, my God, You are Worthy of our praise; You are great and greatly to be praised; You are the Creator of the heaven and the Earth; Your are Mighty; You are Omnipotent, Omnipresent and Omniscient; Your wisdom is unsearchable; The heaven is Your throne, and the earth is Your footstool; Let Your praise continually be in my mouth in Jesus name *(Psalm 34:1)*

ACTION: Although the attributes of God are too numerous to count and more excellent than what we can describe, we should pray that these attributes will help us understand who God is, how we should relate to Him, worship and praise Him and to imitate His character in our lives and reflect His glory to others.

_____

_____

NOVEMBER

Today is NOV 1st ; Day #306, in year 2024.
There are 60 days remaining in year 2024

FAVOR FOR LIFE

SCRIPTURE: *"For His anger is but for a moment, His favor is for life; Weeping may endure for a night, but joy comes in the morning."* ***(Psalms 30:5 NKJV)***

PRAYER: Father, thank You for all Your past blessings and for bringing us into the month of November; in the new season please let us continue to enjoy Your favor, grace, peace, love, joy, protection, provisions, prosperity, excellent health, and divine guidance. Dear Lord, in the remaining 61 days of Year 2024 and henceforth, don't let us do anything to provoke You into anger and let none of us suffer any loss or have any reason to weep or sorrow in Jesus' name

ACTION: Let us pray that we will praise God forever amidst His Saints ***(Psa 52:9)***

_____

_____

Today is NOV 2nd; Day 307 in year 2024.
There are 59 days remaining in year 2024

LOVE GOD WITH CIRCUMCISED HEART AND LIVE

SCRIPTURE: *"The Lord your God will circumcise your hearts and the hearts of your descendants. You will love the Lord your God with all your heart and with all your soul, and you will live." (Deut. 30:6 GW)*

PRAYER: Father, thank You for Jesus Christ and the Holy Spirit through whom our heart's circumcision is made possible *(Rom 2:29; Col. 2:11 GW)*. Oh Lord our God, please let us continue to love You with all our circumcised heart and soul that we may live in Jesus' name *(Deuteronomy 6:5)*

ACTION: Let us pray that, with our circumcised heart we will love God and love our neighbors

Today is NOV 3rd; Day 308 in year 2024.
There are 58 days remaining in the year 2024.

PROPHESIES AND PRAYER CONCERNING EGYPT AND OTHER NATIONS

SCRIPTURE: *"Egypt will be desolate, surrounded by desolate nations, and its cities will be in ruins, surrounded by other ruined cities." **(Ezekiel: 30:7 NLT)***

PRAYER: Father, Your word declares *"For the nation and kingdom which will not serve you shall perish, And those nations shall be utterly ruined." **(Isaiah 60:12 NKJV)***. Please Lord, by Your mercy, let Egypt and all nations serve You in righteousness so that they can be exalted and not suffer reproach **(Pro 14:34)**. Almighty and righteous God, please paralyze, consume by fire and put into ruin nations which remain unrelenting from sins, ungodly, wicked, oppressive, annihilative and persecutive to Christians.

ACTION: Let us pray for global revival that will bring multitude of unbelievers in all nations to turn to Jesus Christ for the salvation of their souls.

_____

_____

Today is NOV 4th; Day 309 in year 2024.
There are 57 days remaining in the year 2024.

BREAKING YOKES AND BURSTING BONDS

SCRIPTURE: *"For it shall come to pass in that day,' Says the Lord of hosts, 'That I will break his yoke from your neck and will burst your bonds; Foreigners shall no more enslave them." (Jeremiah 30:8 NKJV)*

PRAYER: Father, as You delivered the Israelites from the yokes and bonds of king Nebuchadnezzar, please deliver us from all our adversaries by breaking their yokes and bursting their bonds from us in Jesus' name.

ACTION: Pray that the anointing of God in your life will destroy all yokes and bonds in Jesus' name. If need be, get fresh anointing for this purpose *(Isa. 10:27)*

Today is NOV. 5th, Day #310 in year 2024.
There are 56 days remaining in year 2024.

LIFE OF ABUNDANT BLESSINGS FROM THE LORD

SCRIPTURE: *"The Lord your God will give you many blessings in everything you do: You will have many children. Your animals will have many offspring. Your soil will produce many crops. The Lord will again delight in making you as prosperous as he made your ancestors." **(Deut.30:9 GW)***

PRAYER: Father, thank You for the good plan You have for me *(Jer 29:11)*; oh Lord, please give me the grace to obey You totally and to experience Your abundant blessings and prosperity in everything I do in all areas of my life in Jesus mighty name.

ACTION: Let us pray to never neglect or grow weary in doing good works *(Heb 13:16, Gal.6:9)*

_____

_____

Today is NOV 6th; Day 311 in year 2024.
There are 55 days remaining in year 2024.

HELP AND MERCY FROM GOD THE HELPER

SCRIPTURE: *"Hear, O Lord, and have mercy on me; Lord, be my helper!"* ***(Psalms 30:10 NKJV)***

PRAYER: Father, thank You for You are, *"....our refuge and strength, a very present help in trouble"* ***(Psalms 46:1)***. O Lord please hear us when we call on You, have mercy on us and send help to us in Jesus' name

ACTION: Let us pray that the enemy, 'Prince of Persia ', will not be able to delay any help coming to us from the Lord as it was done to Daniel ***(Dan 10: 11-13)***

_____

_____

Today is NOV 7th; Day 312 in year 2024. There are 54 more days remaining in year 2024

GOD'S WORKS ARE MARVELOUSLY GOOD

SCRIPTURE: *"He has made everything beautiful in its time. Also He has put eternity in their hearts, except that no one can find out the work that God does from beginning to end." (Eccl 3:11 NKJV)*

PRAYER: Father, I agree and I echo Job who said, You do *"..great things, and unsearchable, Marvelous things without number." (Job 5:9 NKJV)* and with King David who said *"I will praise thee; for I am fearfully and wonderfully made: marvelous are thy works; and that my soul knoweth right well". (Psalms 139:14 KJV)*. Oh God, in all our works endow us with divine wisdom, excellent and beautiful spirit, and to be eternity focused in Jesus name.

ACTION: Let us pray that all our work will be good and praising God *(Psalm 145:10)*

_____

_____

**Today is NOV 8th; Day 313 in year 2024.
There are 53 days remaining in year 2024**

DELIVER ME O LORD MY REFUGE AND DEFENCE

SCRIPTURE: *"Bow down Your ear to me, Deliver me speedily; Be my rock of refuge, A fortress of defense to save me."* **(Psalms 31:2 NKJV)**

PRAYER: Father, thank You because You are *"my battle axe and weapons of war: ..."* **(Jeremiah 51:20)**. Please Lord, hear me when I call on You; defend and deliver me speedily and keep me safe from all attacks, in Jesus' name.

ACTION: Let us praise God for being our Deliverer, Refuge and Defense

_____

_____

Today is NOV 9th; Day 314 in year 2024
There are 52 days remaining in year 2024

GETTING WISDOM AND UNDERSTANDING FROM GOD

SCRIPTURE: *"Happy is the man who finds wisdom, And the man who gains understanding;"* **(Proverbs 3:13 NKJV)**

PRAYER: Father, Your word declares: *"And God gave Solomon wisdom and exceedingly great understanding, and largeness of heart like the sand on the seashore."* **(I Kings 4:29 NKJV)**
Dear Lord, as You did for Solomon, please give us wisdom and understanding that we, Your people, will live happy and give You all the glory in Jesus name.

ACTION: To be well equipped in building Christ's Church, let's pray that God will fill us with the Spirit of God, in wisdom, in understanding and in knowledge as He did for Bezalel *(Exo 31:1-4)*

Today is November 10th, Day 315 in year 2024.
There are 51 days remaining in year 2024

HARDEN NOT YOUR HEARTS

SCRIPTURE: *"While it is said, Today if ye will hear his voice, harden not your hearts, as in the provocation."* (**Heb. 3:15**)

PRAYER: The end result of hardening the heart to voice of God is disobedience and destruction as exemplified by Pharaoh and the Egyptians *(Exo 14, 1 Sam 6:6)*. Father, please soften the hearts of hearers of the gospel of salvation that they will accept Jesus as their Lord and Savior and not perish as did some Israelites who provoked God to anger in the wilderness *(Deut. 9)*

ACTION: Let's pray to God to give us a new heart and a new mind that will enhance our obedience in doing the will of God *(Ezekiel 11:19)*

**Today is NOV 11th; Day 316 in year 2024.
There are 50 days remaining in year 2024**

"LUKEWARM OR HOT FOR THE LORD?

SCRIPTURE: *"I know your works, that you are neither cold nor hot. I could wish you were cold or hot."* ***(Revelation 3:15 NKJV)***

PRAYER: Father, concerning the Laodicean Church You said *"..because thou art lukewarm, and neither cold nor hot, I will spue thee out of my mouth"* ***(Rev. 3:16)***; Oh Lord God, by Your grace we shall not be like the Laodicean Church; we shall be diligently hot and not lukewarm in serving You in Jesus name. Spirit of lukewarmness we bind you from entering our lives and ministries in Jesus' name.

ACTION: Let us pray to be always hot for the Lord to avoid been spewed out ***(Rev. 3: 15-16)***

_____

_____

Today is NOV 12th; Day 317 in year 2024.
There are 49 days remaining in year 2024

SALVATION THROUGH JESUS CHRIST THE SAVIOR

SCRIPTURE: *"For God so loved the world that He gave His only begotten Son, that whoever believes in Him should not perish but have everlasting life." **(John 3:16 NKJV)***

PRAYER: Father, thank You for making salvation and eternal life possible by grace that requires only confession and repentance from sins and, believing in and accepting Jesus Christ as one's Savior and Lord **(Eph 2:8; John 3:16)**. Lord, Jesus please make us channels by which all unsaved souls are drawn to You for their salvation in Jesus name.

ACTION: Let us pray that God will use us as the channel by which sinners will be drawn to Jesus Christ to receive their salvation **(Rom. 10:14)**

**Today is NOV 13th; Day 318 in year 2024.
There are 48 days remaining in year 2024**

WISDOM FROM ABOVE

SCRIPTURE: *"But the wisdom that is from above is first pure, then peaceable, gentle, willing to yield, full of mercy and good fruits, without partiality and without hypocrisy." (James 3:17 NKJV)*

PRAYER: Father, Your word declares, "Wisdom is the principal thing; therefore get wisdom: and with all thy getting get understanding." *(Pro. 4:7)*. Oh God that gives wisdom liberally *(James 1:5)*, please give us wisdom from above as you gave to: Jesus Christ *(Lk 2:40)*, Bezaleel *(Exo 31:1-3)*, Solomon *(1 Kg 4:29)*, Daniel *(5:14)* etc. May we use the wisdom God gives us to win the world for Him, and fulfill our destinies in Jesus name.

ACTION: Let us pray principally to get wisdom from God as wisdom is the principal thing *(PRO 4:7)*

Today is NOV 14th; Day 319 in year 2024.
There are 47 days remaining in year 2024

PREACHING WITH EXHORTATIONS TO PEOPLE

SCRIPTURE: *"And with many other exhortations he preached to the people." (Luke 3:18 NKJV)*

PRAYER: Father, please give us wisdom, the right words and ways to exhort, encourage and preach the gospel of salvation by Jesus Christ to people that they will hear and willingly surrender their lives to Him in Jesus name

ACTION: Pray for the grace to preach in season and out of season *(2 Tim 4:2)*

Today is NOV 15th; Day 320 in year 2024.
There are 46 days remaining in year 2024

LOVING DARKNESS THAN LIGHT?

SCRIPTURE: *"And this is the condemnation, that the light has come into the world, and men loved darkness rather than light, because their deeds were evil." **(John 3:19 NKJV)**.*

PRAYER: Father, thank You for the gift of Jesus Christ the Sun of Righteousness *(Mal 4:2)* and the Light of the World *(John 8:12, 9:5)*. Lord Jesus please help us to continue to believe in You and abide in You instead of abiding in darkness since You have delivered us from the power of darkness *(John 12:26; Col 1:13)* As the light of the world *(Matt 5:14a)* we shall love light and not darkness and we shall not suffer any condemnation in Jesus' name.

ACTION: AS Jesus is the light of the world let us pray to follow Him so that we will not walk in darkness but will have the light of life. *(John 8:12)*

_____
_____

Today is NOV 16th; Day 321 in year 2024.
There are 45 days remaining in year 2024.

GOD OF 'EXCEEDINGLY ABUNDANTLY'

SCRIPTURE: *"Now to Him who is able to do exceedingly abundantly above all that we ask or think, according to the power that works in us,"* **(Ephesians 3:20 NKJV)**

PRAYER: Omnipotent God, thank You for Your power to multiply and call forth abundance as evident in Your creation of one Adam from whom You have brought forth billions of descendants and we are still counting; You multiplied exceedingly abundantly (EA), only 2 fishes and 5 loaves to feed over 5000 persons with left over of some 12 basketful of food *(John 6:1-14)*; Your anointed EA decree converted the food pantry of the widow of Zarephath from what was to be empty (after her and her son's last meal) to an inexhaustible food tank *(1 Kings 17:8-16)*; oh LORD, please bless me in all areas and make me a blessing in 'exceedingly abundantly' magnitude in Jesus name

ACTION: Let us pray to God to empower us to do excellently and exceed expectation in all our assignments I am expected to do.

_____

_____

**Today is Nov. 17th, Day #322 in year 2024.
There are 44 days remaining in year 2024.**

REIGNING OF THE RIGHTEOUS

SCRIPTURE: *"Behold, a king shall reign in righteousness, and princes shall rule in judgment"* (Isaiah 32:1)

PRAYER: Father, Your word declares, *"When the righteous are in authority, the people rejoice: but when the wicked beareth rule, the people mourn"* ***(Pro. 29:2 KJV)***; oh Lord, please give us righteous and God-fearing kings, rulers and leaders who will do Your will and make nations of the world better and delightful; by your divine power dethrone and eliminate all ungodly, corrupt and wicked rulers

ACTION: As advised by Apostle Paul, pray regularly for *"..kings, and for all that are in authority; that we may lead a quiet and peaceable life in all godliness and honesty." **(1 Tim. 2:3-4)***

Today is NOV 18th; Day 323 in year 2023.
There are 43 days remaining in year 2023

ALL THINGS BELONG TO GOD ALMIGHTY

SCRIPTURE: *"whether Paul or Apollos or Cephas, or the world or life or death, or things present or things to come—all are yours." (I Cor. 3:22 NKJV)*

PRAYER: Father, thank You for Your word declares: *"Yours, O Lord, is the greatness, The power and the glory, The victory and the majesty; For all that is in heaven and in earth is Yours; Yours is the kingdom, O Lord, And You are exalted as head over all." (I Chron. 29:11 NKJV)*.
Amazing God, let all followers of Jesus Christ and their shepherds and other things You have created honor You and glorify You and know that *"You created all things, and for Your pleasure they were created."(Revelation 4:11, KJV)*. Amen.

ACTION: Prayerfully determine to live a life that will give God unlimited pleasures in Jesus name.

_____

_____

**Today is NOV 19th; Day 324 in year 2024.
There are 42 more days remaining in year 2024.**

SERVING GOD HEARTILY TO HIS SATISFACTION

SCRIPTURE: *"And whatever you do, do it heartily, as to the Lord and not to men,"* ***(Col. 3:23 NKJV)***

PRAYER: Father, please let my service to You be driven by the goal to please You rather than to please men; Oh Lord, let the testimony of my service to You be like that of Hezekiah about whom Your word says, *"...he did what was good and right and true before the Lord his God. And in every work that he began in the service ...of God, ..he did it with all his heart. So he prospered."* ***(II Chron. 31:20-21 NKJV)***. Father, by Your grace, I will work for You heartily and prosper highly in Jesus name

ACTION: Let us pray for the grace to do our best to serve God satisfactorily

_____

_____

Today is NOV 20th; Day 325 in year 2024.
There are 41 days remaining in year 2024.

GREAT AND GOOD ATTRIBUTES OF GOD

SCRIPTURE: *"He is the Rock, His work is perfect; For all His ways are justice, A God of truth and without injustice; Righteous and upright is He."* **(Deut.32:4 NKJV)**

PRAYER: Father, thank You for You are great and full of great attributes including, Greatness, the Rock, Perfect in all Your works, Just in all Your ways, Truthful, Righteous, Upright, Holy, Faithful, Merciful, Mighty, Peaceful, etc. Oh Lord, please let us continue to be beneficiaries of all Your good and great attributes in Jesus name.

ACTION: Thank God for all His attributes which are great and perfect,

_____

_____

**Today is NOV 21st; Day 326 in year 2022.
There are 40 days remaining in year 2024**

REWARDS FOR WAITING AND SEEKING GOD

SCRIPTURE: *"The Lord is good to those who wait for Him, To the soul who seeks Him." (Lam. 3:25 NKJV)*

PRAYER: Father, Your word declares: *"But they that wait upon the LORD shall renew their strength; they shall mount up with wings as eagles; they shall run, and not be weary; and they shall walk, and not faint." (Isaiah 40:31, KJV)* and that: *"...let the heart of them rejoice that seek the LORD." (Psa. 105:3b)*; Dear Lord, I receive Your grace to wait on You without wavering and to seek Your face faithfully, and I receive the blessings that appertain to doing so in Jesus name.

ACTION: Let us pray for God's grace to give us the patience we need to achieve our goals in all we do.

_____

_____

Today is NOV 22nd; Day 327 in year 2024. There are 39 days remaining in year 2024

GOOD TO HOPE AND WAIT FOR SALVATION OF GOD

SCRIPTURE: *"It is good that one should hope and wait quietly For the salvation of the Lord."* **(Lamentations 3:26 NKJV)**

PRAYER: Father, thank You for the souls You have already redeemed and saved. Oh Lord, by Your love and grace please let those yet unsaved put their hope on You and by faith wait and turn to You quietly (but quickly) for their salvation in Jesus name.

ACTION: Let us pray that nothing will delay the salvation of those we are ministering to or praying for to receive Jesus Christ as their Savior.

Today is NOV 23rd; Day 328 in year 2022.
There are 38 days remaining in year 2022

PLUNDERING THE STRONG MAN CALLS FIRST FOR HIS PARALYSIS

SCRIPTURE: *"No one can enter a strong man's house and plunder his goods, unless he first binds the strong man. And then he will plunder his house." **(Mark 3:27 NKJV)***

PRAYER: Father, please deliver us from spiritual blasphemy akin to that of the scribes who said about Jesus Christ, *"...He hath Beelzebub, and by the prince of the devils casteth he out devils. **(Mark 3:22)**.* Dear Lord, give us the grace to live holy and be filled with the Holy Spirit by which we can dispossess devils out of the bodies or souls of men

ACTION: Let us pray to God to shield us against all stubborn attackers.

Today is NOV 24th, Day 329 in year 2024. There are 37 days remaining in year 2024

NEVER DENY OR DELAY HELPING YOUR NEIGHBOR

SCRIPTURE: *"If you can help your neighbor now, don't say, "Come back tomorrow, and then I'll help you."* ***(Proverbs 3:28 NLT)***

PRAYER: Father, please give me the grace to obey You by loving You and loving my neighbors with all my heart and soul according to Your great commandments as in ***Matt. 22:37-39 NKJV***. Dear Lord, empower me to render needed help timely to my neighbors in Jesus name

ACTION: Let us prayerfully render needed help to our household and neighborhood members

_____

_____

Today is NOV 25th, Day 330 in year 2024.
There are 36 days remaining in year 2024

ANOINTING ON SHADRACH, MESHACH AND ABED-NEGO

SCRIPTURE: *"Therefore I make a decree that any people, nation, or language which speaks anything amiss against the God of Shadrach, Meshach, and Abed-Nego shall be cut in pieces, and their houses shall be made an ash heap; because there is no other God who can deliver like this."* **(Dan. 3:29 NKJV)**

PRAYER: Father, please continue to be my God, let me live holy and let me carry Your anointing for divine protection as You did for Shadrach, Meshach, and Abed-Nego who were thrown into furnace of fire and they came out unhurt and were promoted *(Dan Chap3)*

ACTION: Let us prayerfully claim the word of God in *Psa 105:15 & 1 Chron 16:22*

**Today is NOV 26th, Day 331 in year 2024.
There are 35 days remaining in year 2024**

JESUS MUST INCREASE AND I MUST DECREASE

SCRIPTURE: *"He must become greater and greater, and I must become less and less." (John 3:30 NLT)*

PRAYER: Father, thank Your for Your Son Jesus Christ, the Messiah and Savior of the world. Oh God, please let Jesus be greater and greater in our lives every day for, *"..He is the head of the body, the church, who is the beginning, the firstborn from the dead, that in all things He may have the preeminence."(Colossians 1:18 NKJV)*. Lord Jesus, You are the good Shepherd and we are the sheep, You must increase (in fame, reputation; in miracles, in conversion of souls through the spread of the Gospel, etc.), while I must decrease in Jesus name

ACTION: Let us endeavor do everything to the glory of God *(1 Cor 10:31)*

_____

_____

Today is NOV 27th, Day 332 in year 2024.
There are 34 days remaining in year 2024

REJOICING IN THE LORD AND PRAISE HIM RIGHTEOUSLY

SCRIPTURE: *"Rejoice in the Lord, O you righteous! For praise from the upright is beautiful." **(Psalms 33:1 NKJV)***

PRAYER: Father, in this season and forever let sorrows be far from us and let us always have reasons to rejoice righteously in You according to the following scriptures: *"I will praise the LORD according to his righteousness: and will sing praise to the name of the LORD most high." **(Psalms 7:17, KJV)***
*"And my tongue shall speak of thy righteousness and of thy praise all the day long" **(Psalms 35:28, KJV)***
*"Open to me the gates of righteousness; I will go through them, And I will praise the Lord." **(Psalms 118:19 NKJV)***

ACTION: Let us pray that the joy of the Lord will continue to be our strength *(Neh 1:10)*

_____
_____

Today is NOV 28th, Day 333 in year 2024.
There are 33 days remaining in year 2024.

PERVERSE VERSUS UPRIGHT PERSONS

SCRIPTURE: *"For the perverse person is an abomination to the Lord, But His secret counsel is with the upright." (Proverbs 3:32 NKJV)*

PRAYER: Father, according to *Proverbs 3:33*, perverseness (or wickedness) attracts curses from You while uprightness (or to be just) attracts blessings from You); please give me the grace to live uprightly rather than perversely such that my home shall be blessed perpetually and never cursed in Jesus' name

ACTION: Let us pray that God will keep harmful and perverse people away from us

_____

_____

Today is NOV 29th, Day 334 in year 2024.
There are 32 days remaining in the year 2024.

CALLING TO BE SHOWN GREAT AND MIGHTY THINGS BY JESUS CHRIST

SCRIPTURE: *"Call to Me, and I will answer you, and show you great and mighty things, which you do not know.'" **(Jer. 33:3 NKJV)***

PRAYER: Father, thank You for Your faithfulness to Your promise to answer me whenever I call on You. Dear Lord, please give me wisdom from above and empower me to live holy, love You the more, serve You more diligently and to know and do Your will faithfully all the times in Jesus' name.

ACTION: Let us pray that God who reveals the deep and secret things will give us divine revelations that will lead to hidden riches of dark places *(Dan 2:22)*

Today is NOV 30th, Day 335 in year 2024.
There are 31 days remaining in year 2024

SENT BY GOD TO SPEAK HIS WORD BY THE SPIRIT

SCRIPTURE: *"The one that God has sent speaks God's words. God has given his Spirit to fill that person completely." (John 3:34 EASY)*

PRAYER: Father, thank You for the gift of Your Word (Jesus Christ) and Your word (the Holy Bible), as well as the gift of the Holy Spirit *(John 1:1; Luke 11:13; 1 Cor 12)*. Please LORD, empower us to declare Your Word and Your word accurately with the help of the Holy Spirit in Jesus name.

ACTION: Let us pray that any time we are opportune or required to talk about God and His Church, that the Holy Spirit will teach us in that very hour what to say and how to say it *(Luke 12: 11-12)."*

_____

_____

DECEMBER

Today is DEC 1st, Day 336 in year 2024.
There are 30 days remaining in year 2024

GOD'S GRACIOUS GIFTS

SCRIPTURE: *"And he lifted his eyes and saw the women and children, and said, "Who are these with you?" So he said, "The children whom God has graciously given your servant." (Genesis 33:5 NKJV)*

PRAYER: Father, thank You because every good and perfect gift comes from You *(James 1:17)*. Children are not only good, gifts, they are also gracious gifts from God. Dear LORD, as You graciously gave Jacob and other people like us many children, please do the same for those who are looking for children in Jesus name. Father, please let the lives of all our children be Godly, gracious and glorious in Jesus name.

ACTION: Pray for perfect gifts from the LORD *(James 1:17)*

Today is DEC 2nd, Day 337 in year 2024.
There are 29 days remaining in year 2024

PROMISE OF PEACE FOR THE PEOPLE

SCRIPTURE: *"But I will heal this city and restore it to health. I will heal its people, and I will give them peace and security."* ***(Jer. 33:6 GW)***

PRAYER: Father, please heal and restore peace and security to all our cities as You revealed (via Prophet Jeremiah) You would do for Judah and Israel ***(Jer.33:1-6)***. Also, Lord, help us to do our part by heeding Your counsel: *"If My people who are called by My name will humble themselves, and pray and seek My face, and turn from their wicked ways, then I will hear from heaven, and will forgive their sin and heal their land."* ***(II Chron. 7:14 NKJV)***

ACTION: Let us praise Jesus for being the Prince of Peace ***(Isaiah 9:6)***

Today is DEC 3rd, Day 338 in year 2024.
There are 28 days remaining in year 2024

WORDS OF MAN ARE INEFFECTIVE WITHOUT GOD'S APPROVAL

SCRIPTURE: *"Who is he who speaks, and it comes to pass, When the Lord has not commanded it?"* **(Lamentations 3:37 NKJV).**

PRAYER: Father, Your word declares that *"Every word of God is pure; He is a shield to those who put their trust in Him."* **(Pro. 30:5 NKJV)** and that, *"The statutes of the Lord are right, rejoicing the heart; The commandment of the Lord is pure, enlightening the eyes;"* **(Psalms 19:8 NKJV).** Please Lord, let every word spoken about me be filtered through Your pure word, statutes and commandments such that all those are curses and negative words about me backfire or cancelled while those that are positive words are upheld and allowed to manifest in Jesus name.

ACTION: Let us guide and tongues and pray not to say anything God has not ordained.

_____
_____

Today is DEC 4th, Day 339 in the year 2024.
There are 27 days remaining in year 2024.

PROMISE OF GOD TO HAVE ALL SINS AND INIQUITIES PARDONED

SCRIPTURE: *"I will cleanse them from all their iniquity by which they have sinned against Me, and I will pardon all their iniquities by which they have sinned and by which they have transgressed against Me." **(Jeremiah 33:8 NKJV)***

PRAYER: Father, Your word declares *"If You, Lord, should mark iniquities, ...who could stand? But there is forgiveness with You,."**(Psa. 130:3-4 NKJV)***. By Your mercy oh Lord, please let repentance revival take place in our nations to provoke You to pardon all sins and iniquities as You promised to do for Judah and Israel ***(Jer. 33:1-9)***

ACTION: Sing the Hymn: WHO CAN WASH AWAY MY SIN, NOTHING BUT THE BLOOD OF JESUS ...

_____

_____

Today is DEC 5th, Day 340 in the year 2024.
There are 26 days remaining in year 2024

MANASSEH'S GRIEVIOUS MISTAKE AND MESS

SCRIPTURE: *"But Manasseh led the people of Judah and Jerusalem to do even more evil than the pagan nations that the Lord had destroyed when the people of Israel entered the land." (2 Ch ron. 33:9 NLT)*

PRAYER: Father, in our countries and nations give us Godly leaders who will show good examples of serving You faithfully and steadily instead of leaders like Manasseh who by vacillating between serving God and worshipping of idols encouraged people of Judah and Jerusalem into doing things abominable to God *(2 kings 21:1-16, KJV)*

ACTION: Pray that God will make us leaders that will lead people to Salvation not to sins.

_____

_____

Today is DEC 6th, Day 341 in year 2024.
There are 25 days remaining in year 2024

LOOKING CLOSELY AT OUR WAYS TO RETURN TO THE LORD

SCRIPTURE: *"Let us look closely at our ways and examine them and then return to the Lord."* ***(Lam. 3:40 GW)***

PRAYER: Father Your thoughts and ways are perfect and much superior and better than that of man ***(Isa 58:8-9, Ps 18:30)***; Oh Lord, help us and give us the courage to self-examine our ways and turn away from sinful and unrighteous ways and return to You in Jesus name. Oh Lord, I also echo the psalmist to pray as follows: *"Make your ways known to me, O Lord, and teach me your paths."* ***(Psalms 25:4 GW)***; *"Teach me your way, O Lord. Lead me on a level path because I have enemies who spy on me."* ***(Psalms 27:11 GW).***

ACTION: Let us prayerfully focus our heart on reverential fearing of God." ***(Psalms 86:11 GW)***

_____

_____

Today is DEC 7th, Day 342 in year 2024.
There are 24 days remaining in year 2024

PRAISING AND THANKING GOD PERPETUALLY

SCRIPTURE: *"I will thank the Lord at all times. My mouth will always praise him."* **(Psalms 34:1 GW)**

PRAYER: Father, thank You for all You have done, still doing and will still do for me. Oh Lord, since Your word declares *"Pray without ceasing"* **(1 Thess 5:17)**, please don't let me stop or slack in praying to You, thanking You, praising You and praying to You, perpetually in Jesus name.

ACTION: Like David, Let us pray that praising God will continually be in our mouth **(Psalm 34:1)**

_____

_____

Today is DEC 8th, Day 343 in the year 2024.
There are 23 days remaining in year 2024

BAD VERSUS GOOD BOASTING

SCRIPTURE: *"My soul will boast about the Lord. Those who are oppressed will hear it and rejoice." **(Psalms 34:2 GW)***

PRAYER: Father, please deliver us from bad and evil boastings such as boasting of serving graven images and worshipping idols *(Psa 97:7)*; instead let our boasting be like that of the Psalmist who declares *"In God we boast all the day long, and praise thy name for ever. Selah" **(Psalms 44:8)***. By Your grace oh Lord I will not be one of the 'boasters' that will serve as the sign of the last days of perilous time *(2 Tim. 3:1-5)*

ACTION: Let us pray that our boasting will be only about the LORD *(1 Corinthians 1:31 NLT)*

Today is DEC 9th, Day 344 in year 2024.
There are 22 days remaining in year 2024

POWER OF UNITED AND CORPORATE PRAISE

SCRIPTURE: *"Oh, magnify the Lord with me, And let us exalt His name together." **(Psa. 34:3 NKJV)***

PRAYER: Oh Lord God let us be united and be of one accord in praising You and worshipping Your Majesty so that the earth will yield its increase unto us and we shall be abundantly blessed in Jesus name **(Psalms 67:5-7 NKJV)**.

ACTION: Let us emulate Paul and Silas by participating actively in praising God **(Acts 16)**

Today is DEC 10th, Day 345 in year 2024.
There are 21 days remaining in year 2024

GOD THAT ANSWERS PRAYER AND ALLAYS FEARS

SCRIPTURE: *"I prayed to the Lord, and he answered me. He freed me from all my fears." **(Psalms 34:4 NLT)***

PRAYER: Father, thank You for Your faithfulness in answering our prayers according to Your promise ***(Jer 3:33; Matt 7:7-8).***
Please Lord, help us to put our trust in You to lead us to be free from fear as You did for the Israelites at the Red Sea: *"And he led them on safely, so that they feared not: but the sea overwhelmed their enemies"* ***(Psalms 78:53)***

ACTION: Pray that the perfect love of God that saved us and is in us will cast all fears away ***(1 John 4:18)***

**Today is DEC 11th, Day 346 in year 2024.
There are 20 days remaining in year 2024**

GOD OF A SECOND CHANCE

SCRIPTURE: *"Now the Lord descended in the cloud and stood with him there and proclaimed the name of the Lord." (Exodus 34:5 NKJV)*

PRAYER: Father, thank You for Your faithfulness, mercy and compassion for giving the Israelites a second chance to receive the 2 tables of the 10 commandments after Moses broke the first set due to anger on Mount Sinai. Lord, please give us the grace never to break your commandments in Jesus name *(Exp 34)*

Dear Lord, wherever I have erred in doing Your will please have mercy on me and give me the opportunity to make amends and do what is right in your sight in Jesus name.

ACTION: Let's pray to God to restore to us any blessings we might have missed or lost *(Joel 2:25)*

Today is DEC 12th, Day 347 in year 2024. There are 19 days remaining in year 2024

GOD THAT HEARS PRAYERS OF ALL PEOPLE

SCRIPTURE: *"This poor man cried out, and the Lord heard him, And saved him out of all his troubles.* By *(Psalms 34:6 NKJV)*

PRAYER: Father, thank You because all flesh (poor and rich) can come to You and You hear their prayers *(Psa 65:1-2 NKJV)*. Oh Lord, please teach us to live holy and pray aright and save us from all troubles.

ACTION: Lert us thank and praise God for His promise to answer us when we call on Him *(Jer. 33:3)*

_____

_____

Today is DEC 13th, Day 348 in year 2024.
There are 18 days remaining in the year 2024.

BENEFITS OF FEARING THE FATHER

SCRIPTURE: *"The angel of the Lord encamps all around those who fear Him, And delivers them."* **(Psalms 34:7 NKJV).**

PRAYER: Father, please give me the grace and the commitment to fear You and to enjoy the benefits that appertain for so doing, including:
(1) surrounded by Angels for total deliverance,
(2) Enhanced wisdom and knowledge *(Job 28:28, Pro. 1:7)*,
(3) Prolonged life *(Pro 10:27)*,
(4) Enjoy God's HELP AND mercy forever *(Psa 115:11 Psa 118:4)*,
(5) Lacks nothing good *(Psa 34:9)*

ACTION: Let us serve God with reverential fear that can fetch us rewards including wisdom *(Psa 111:10)*

Today is Dec 14th, Day #349 in the year 2024.
There are 17 days to end year 2024.

GOODNESS OF GOD

SCRIPTURE: *"O taste and see that the LORD is good: blessed is the man that trusteth in him." **(Psalm 34:8, KJV)**.*

PRAYER: Father, thank You for You are the epitome of goodness *(**Matt. 19:17; Mark 10:18; Luke 18:19**)* and Your word in ***James 1:17*** declares: *"Every good gift and every perfect gift is from above, and comes down from the Father of lights, with whom there is no variation or shadow of turning."* Oh Lord, my trust is in You, please let Your goodness and mercy follow me and my household to the end of year 2023 and beyond in Jesus' name.

ACTION: Praise God and call on Him daily to claim the blessings in ***Psalm 86:5,15***.

_____

_____

Today is DEC 15th, Day 350 in year 2024.
There are 16 days remaining in the year 2024.

COVETOUS SHEPHERD OR CHRISTLY SHEPHERD?

SCRIPTURE: *"therefore, O shepherds, hear the word of the Lord!" (Ezekiel 34:9 NKJV)*

PRAYER: Father, please give us Godly / Christly shepherds (Pastors) who will hear and obey Your word and do Your will instead of covetous (greedy) shepherds laden with corruption, apostasy, and feeding of themselves instead of their flocks akin to those in Israel that Ezekiel prophesied against *(Ezek. 34:1-9)*. Oh Lord, let all shepherds (Pastors) be like the Good Shepherd *(John 10:1-15)*

ACTION: Pray for all Church leaders to hear from God and do His will

_____

_____

**Today is DEC 16th, Day 351 in year 2024.
There are 15 days remaining in year 2024.**

HELP FROM HEAVEN

SCRIPTURE: *"until the Lord looks down on us from heaven. He will see us and he will help us."* ***(Lamentations 3:50 EASY)***

PRAYER: Father, thank You for Your loving kindness and multitude of mercies that You have towards us ***(Psa 36:10; 69:13)***; please give us the grace to do like the Psalmist who said : *"I will lift up mine eyes unto the hills, from whence cometh my help"* ***(Psalms 121:1)***. As we look on to You, please Lord, look down on us from heaven in our wretched circumstances and help us in Jesus' name.

ACTION: Pray to serve and seek God with a loyal heart and a willing mind together with our family.

_____

_____

Today is DEC 17th, Day 352 in year 2024.
There are 14 days remaining in year 2024.

ATTACK, O LORD, MY ATTACKERS

SCRIPTURE: *"Lord, please attack those people who are attacking me. Fight against those people who are fighting against me."* ***(Psalms 35:1 EASY)***

PRAYER: Father, the LORD of host, my battle axe and weapon of war, ***(Jer 51:20)***; please attack, fight against and paralyze all those who attack and fight against us in Jesus name.

ACTION: Pray that God will fight for you such that all your attackers will become your admirers.

Today is DEC 18th, Day 353 in year 2024.
There are 13 days remaining in the year 2024.

HUNTED BY THE ENEMIES?

SCRIPTURE: *"Those who were my enemies for no reason hunted me like a bird." (Lam.3:52 GW)*

PRAYER: Father, Your word declares, *"…..When the enemy shall come in like a flood, the Spirit of the LORD shall lift up a standard against him". (Isaiah 59:19).* Oh Spirit of Lord God, please lift up a standard against all my enemies who hunt after me in Jesus name

ACTION: Pray that all Hunters for your life will end up seeking your help

_____

_____

Today is DEC 19th, Day 354 in year 2024.
There are 12 days remaining in the year 2024.

STRENGTHENING HANDS AND WEAK KNEES

SCRIPTURE: *"Strengthen limp hands. Steady weak knees." (Isai 35:3 GW)*

PRAYER: Father, Your word declares, *".... God is our refuge and strength, a very present help in trouble"* ***(Psalms 46:1)***, Oh Lord God, please strengthen us spiritually and physically wherever we are weak in Jesus' name.

ACTION: Pray that God will perfect the functionality of every part of your body ***(Psa 138:8)***

_____

_____

Today is DEC 20th, Day 355 in year 2024.
There are 11 days remaining in year 2024.

DERANGE OH LORD MY POTENTIAL DESTROYERS

SCRIPTURE: *"Cause the people who want to kill me to become ashamed. Chase away the people who want to hurt me, so that they become confused."* ***(Psalms 35:4 EASY)***

PRAYER: Father, please let all potential enemies who are determined to kill and destroy me suffer derangement and delusions and have no choice but flee before me in Jesus' name ***(Deut 28:7)***

ACTION: Pray and thank God for always fighting your battle

Today is DEC 21st, Day 356 in year 2024.
There are 10 days remaining in the year 2024.

WARNING AGAINST ALCOHOLIC WINE

SCRIPTURE: *"Then I set before the sons of the house of the Rechabites bowls full of wine, and cups; and I said to them, "Drink wine." But they said, "We will drink no wine, for Jonadab the son of Rechab, our father, commanded us, saying, 'You shall drink no wine, you nor your sons, forever."* **(Jeremiah. 35:5-6 NKJV).**

PRAYER: Father, as the sons of house of Rechabites obeyed their father not to drink alcoholics wine, please give us the grace to obey You by abstaining from alcoholic wine for Your word declares. *"Wine is a mocker, strong drink is raging and whosoever is deceived thereby is not wise".* **(Pro, 20:1)** and, *"Give strong drink not unto him that is ready to perish, and wine unto those that be of heavy hearts".* **(Pro. 31:6).**
Oh Lord, help us to be wise and let not that which we eat and drink kill us in Jesus name

ACTION: Pray and avoid alcohol or anything that can defile you

_____
_____

Today is DEC 22nd, Day 357 in year 2024.
There are 9 days remaining in the year 2024.

TURNING THE TIDE

SCRIPTURE: *"Then the lame shall leap like a deer, And the tongue of the dumb sing. For waters shall burst forth in the wilderness, And streams in the desert."* **(Isaiah 35:6 NKJV)**

PRAYER: Father, Your word declares, *"When the LORD turned again the captivity of Zion, We were like them that dream. Then was our mouth filled with laughter, And our tongue with singing: Then said they among the heathen, The LORD hath done great things for them."* **(Psalm 126:1-2 KJV)**. Dear Lord, please let this era be the time and season You will turn the tides in our favor in all areas: from lameness to leaping; dumbness to talking; dryness to showers of blessings; scarcity to surplus, sorrows to singing joyfully; failure to success; sickness to excellent healing; barrenness to fruitfulness; poverty to prosperity; sinfulness to holiness in Jesus name.

ACTION: Pray that the tide will turn in your favor in all aspects and God will be glorified.

_____
_____

Today is DEC 23rd, Day 358 in year 2024.
There are 8 days remaining in year 2024

GOD OF ENCOURAGEMENT

SCRIPTURE: *"You drew near on the day I called on You, And said, "Do not fear!"* ***(Lam 3:57 NKJV)***

PRAYER: Father, thank You for Your word declares, *"Fear thou not; for I am with thee: be not dismayed; for I am thy God: I will strengthen thee; yea, I will help thee; yea, I will uphold thee with the right hand of my righteousness"* ***(Isaiah 41:10)***; and to *"Be strong and of a good courage....for the LORD thy God, he it is that doth go with thee; he will not fail thee, nor forsake thee."* ***(Deut. 31:6)***. Oh God Emmanuel, please encourage me, protect me, provide for me, prosper me and perfect everything concerning me and my family in Jesus name

ACTION: Prayerfully obey God's injunction to *"Fear not"* because of His presence with you.

_____

_____

**Today is DEC 24th, Day 359 in year 2024.
There are 7 days remaining in year 2024.**

LORD HAD PLED FOR AND RECLAIMED MY LIFE

SCRIPTURE: *"O Lord, You have pleaded the case for my soul; You have redeemed my life."* ***(Lam. 3:58 NKJV)***

PRAYER: Father, Your word declares, *"The LORD redeems the soul of His servants, And none of those who trust in Him shall be condemned"* ***(Psa 34:22)***. Oh God, the Redeemer of my soul, please let those who are yet to surrender their lives to You, run to You now (before it's too late) for the forgiveness of their sins and redemption of their souls in Jesus' name.

ACTION: Give thanks to God for counting you worthy to be redeemed at the cost of His only begotten son, Jesus Christ

Today is DEC 25th, Day 360 in year 2024.
There are 6 days remaining in year 2024.

JOYFUL IN JESUS

SCRIPTURE: *"And my soul shall be joyful in the Lord; It shall rejoice in His salvation." **(Psa. 35:9 NKJV)***.

PRAYER: Father, thank You for the gift of Your Son Jesus Christ whose birthday we celebrate on Christmas Day today ***(Isa 9:6, John 3:16)***. Father, please let me continue to be joyful and rejoicing in Jesus Christ my Redeemer and the God of my salvation ***(Hab. 3:18)*** in Jesus' name.

ACTION: Give special praise and thanks to God for seeing another Christmas Day today.

**Today is DEC 26th, Day 361 in year 2024.
There are 5 days remaining in year 2024**

GOD KNOWS ALL BAD PLOTS ABOUT ME

SCRIPTURE: *"You know all the bad things that they did to me. And you know about all the bad things that they want to do to me."* **(Lam. 3:60 EASY)**

PRAYER: Omniscient God, please avenge for me and shield me against all evil plots. Let all bad things aimed at me go back to the senders in Jesus's name.

ACTION: Pray that GOD will reverse all evil and bad things against you to become blessings in **(Gen. 50:20)**

_____

_____

Today is DEC 27th, Day 362 in year 2024.
There are 4 days remaining in the year 2024.

HELP FROM GOD FOR KING HEZEKIAH

SCRIPTURE: *"When King Hezekiah had ruled Judah for 14 years, King Sennacherib of Assyria attacked Judah with his army. He took all the strong cities in Judah for himself." (Isaiah 36:1 EASY)*

PRAYER: Father, please help me overcome my attackers as You did for king Hezekiah who prayed to You when his territory was invaded by king Sennacherib of Assyria. One night, *"...the Lord's angel went to the camp of the Assyrian army. He killed 185,000 of their soldiers...and...* One day, Sennacherib was worshipping his god Nisrok, in Nisrok's temple. Two of Sennacherib's sons, Adrammelech and Sharezer, went in and they killed him with their sword...." *(Isa. 37:36, 38 EASY)*

ACTION: Praise and thank God for being Your Present help *(Psa. 46:1)*

**Today is DEC 28th, Day #363 in the year 2024.
There are 3 days remaining in year 2024.**

GIFTED BY GOD AND CHOSEN TO BUILD HOUSE OF GOD

SCRIPTURE: *"Then Moses called Bezalel and Aholiab, and every gifted artisan in whose heart the Lord had put wisdom, everyone whose heart was stirred, to come and do the work." (Exodus 36:2 NKJV).*

PRAYER: Father, what a privilege and great blessing to have the opportunity to work for You *(Exo 23:25)*; as You did for Bezalel, Aholiab and other artisans, please let me be among those gifted, qualified, equipped with wisdom, the willingness and stirred heart to participate in building Your Church of which You said: *"...I will build my church; and the gates of hell shall not prevail against it. (Matthew 16:18)*.

ACTION: Let's prayerfully consider how to use our God-given skills to advance the Gospel

_____

_____

**Today is DEC 29th, Day 364 in year 2024.
There are 2 days remaining in year 2024.**

"WICKEDNESS OF THE WICKED

SCRIPTURE: *"He speaks wicked things to deceive people. He does nothing that is wise or good."* **(Psalms 36:3 EASY)**

PRAYER: Father, Your word declares, *"...Wickedness proceeds from the wicked..."* **(I Samuel 24:13 NKJV).**
Oh Lord, please deliver us from wicked people and their sinful and anti God behavior; please let their wickedness come to an end in Jesus name **(Psa. 36:1-3; Psa 7:9)**

ACTION: Pray to *"..not enter the path of the wicked, And, ..to not walk in the way of evil"* **(Pro 14:4)**.

Today is DEC 30th, Day 365 in year 2024. There is 1 day remaining in year 2024.

DIVINE 'TIT FOR TAT'

SCRIPTURE: *"Pay them back, Lord, for all the evil they have done"* ***(Lamentations 3:64 NLT)***

PRAYER: Father, Your word declares, *"...Whoso rewardeth evil for good, evil shall not depart from his house"*, ***(Pro. 17:13, KJV)***. Oh Righteous Lord, fight for me and pay them back with evil those who have persistently rewarded my good done to them with evil; as well as those I have never harmed, who *"...have hunted me down like a bird. Threw me into a pit, and dropped stones on me."* ***(Lam. 3:52-53 NLT)***.

ACTION: Let God fight for you so that you can have your peace ***(Exo 14:14)***

_____
_____

**Today is DEC 31st, Day 366th in year 2024.
There is 0 day remaining in year 2024.**

ALPHA AND OMEGA

SCRIPTURE: *"Your goodness is higher than the highest mountains. Your fairness is deeper than the deepest ocean. Lord, you protect people and animals." **(Psa 36: 6, EASY)***

PRAYER: Father, thank You for the journey so far this year. Oh Lord, please let this last day of Year 2024 bring me gladness, joy, peace, restoration of any lost blessings and manifestation of any blessings meant for this year that has not materialized so far

ACTION: Sing 7 praise /thanksgiving songs to God for keeping you safe throughout year 2024 and pray that Jesus Christ, the Alpha and Omega will see you safe throughout the new year 2025 *(Rev 1:8)*

www.ingramcontent.com/pod-product-compliance
Lightning Source LLC
Chambersburg PA
CBHW071259110426
42743CB00042B/1103